POWER BASICS®

American Government

Robert Taggart

J. WESTON
WALCH
PUBLISHER

JWW282   v1.02

POWER BASICS ®

Senior Author	Robert Taggart
Editorial Director	Susan Blair
Project Manager/Senior Production Editor	Maggie Jones
Project Editor	Erica Varney
Director of Marketing	Jeff Taplin
Interior Design	Mark Sayer
Cover Design	Roman Laszok
Typesetting	Sheila Russell
	Mark Sayer
	Ian Weidner
Editorial Staff	Elizabeth Lynch
	Richard Lynch
	Holly Moirs
	Kate O'Halloran
	Mary Rich

ISBN 978-0-8251-5652-6

Copyright © 1998, 2005

J. Weston Walch, Publisher

10200 Jefferson Blvd. | Culver City, CA 90232

www.socialstudies.com/walch

Printed in the United States of America

J. WESTON

WALCH

PUBLISHER

Table of Contents

Table of Contents, *continued*

To the Student

Welcome to the *Power Basics ® American Government*. This book will teach you the basics of federal, state, and local government in our country. You will learn about how the government of the United States developed over time, what it is like compared to other governments, and how it works today in everyday life.

Unit 1: What is Government? tells about the three forms of government—democracy, monarchy, and dictatorship. These forms of government are being used in countries around the world today. Learning about how they work will help you understand the world around you.

In **Unit 2: The Constitutional Framework,** you will study the basic principles and parts of the U.S. Constitution. You will learn about the three parts of the Constitution and how the Constitution creates a balance of power in our government.

Unit 3: Political Parties and Voting will introduce you to the political parties in the United States. Political parties play an important role in any representative democracy. You will learn about political parties and how they work. You will also learn the voting duties of a responsible citizen in this unit.

In **Unit 4: The Federal Government,** you will learn about the executive, legislative, and judicial branches of the national government. You will learn how each branch is set up, what its duties are, and how separation of powers works.

In **Unit 5: The Presidential Election Process,** you will discover how the president and vice president of the United States are elected. The president and vice president are two of the most important people in the U.S. government. You will learn the process of a presidential election, from voting in primaries to the duties of the electoral college.

Unit 6: State Government will introduce you to the way state government is set up and how it works. You will learn the responsibilities of state government and what services state governments provide for their citizens.

Unit 7: Local Government will introduce you to local governments and how they work. You will find out about both county government and municipal (city and town) government. You will also learn about the duties of these types of government and what they provide.

Power Basics American Government has many special features that make learning easier. "Tips" give you hints on ways to master the ideas and facts in the text. "In Real Life" sections give you examples of real-life events and people that will help you relate to the information you are learning. "Think About It" questions ask you to look at facts in a new way. And the "Words to Know" section at the start of each lesson includes important new terms introduced in the book. The words appear in the Glossary at the end of the book. Finally, the Appendixes at the back of the book include further useful information.

As you move through *Power Basics American Government,* you will understand how our government works and gain the knowledge you need to become an informed and responsible citizen. We hope you enjoy this material as you learn.

UNIT 1

What Is Government?

LESSON 1: Forms of Government

GOAL: To learn what government is and some forms it may take

WORDS TO KNOW

anarchists	government
anarchy	majority
citizen	monarch
constitutional monarchy	monarchy
democracy	prime minister
despotism	totalitarian state
dictator (tyrant, despot)	totalitarianism
dictatorship	tyranny

What Is a Government?

Suppose you start a neighborhood group with people who live on your block. You hold your first meeting. It is disorderly. Your neighbors have good ideas, but no one is listening. Everybody wants to solve problems in the neighborhood, but nobody is working together. Nothing is getting done. Some people are angry. They are shouting at each other. A few people are standing up to leave.

What can you do? You need a plan for managing, or running, your group.

Groups of people always work better together if they have a system or a plan. The group may be small, like a club or a business. Or it may be large, like a city, a state, or a country. A plan always helps. A plan or system for managing or ruling a city, state, or country is called a **government**.

■ PRACTICE 1: What Is a Government?

Circle the letter of the correct answer to each question below.

1. Which statement is TRUE about having a plan for running a group?
   a. It will not work with a small group.
   b. It works better with more people.
   c. It helps people work together.
   d. It will make people angry.

2. What is a government?
   a. a system for managing a city, state, or country
   b. a club made up of ten or fewer members
   c. a disorderly meeting
   d. a system for managing a small club

Types of Government

You and your friends decide to find a plan to run your neighborhood group. Three possible plans are listed below. Most governments are also based on these same plans.

PLAN 1: Each member gets to vote on every decision. Everybody goes along with the **majority** (the side with the most votes).

A country with this system is called a **democracy**.

PLAN 2: The leader of the group is a bully. Everybody does what the bully says.

A country with this system is called a **dictatorship**.

PLAN 3: The richest, most powerful person gets to tell everybody what to do. This person's children will lead the group some day.

A country with this system is called a **monarchy**.

A situation in which there is no plan or government is called **anarchy**. People who want no government are called **anarchists**.

■ PRACTICE 2: Types of Government

Circle the letter of the type(s) of government that each statement describes.

1. "You have to give the club a dollar every week. That is how we voted."
   a. democracy
   b. dictatorship
   c. monarchy
   d. anarchy

2. "You have to give the club a dollar every week. Our leader, Joe, says so." (*Hint*: There are two correct answers.)
   a. democracy
   b. dictatorship
   c. monarchy
   d. anarchy

Democracy

The members of your neighborhood group are holding a meeting. First, they discuss whether or not to start a recycling project. They talk about who they want to be the leader of the group. Every member who wants to speak up gets a chance. Then the group votes. Every member votes. Each member's vote is equally important.

After the vote is counted, everybody goes along with the majority's decision. The majority is the side with the most votes.

This neighborhood group is run like a *democracy.*

These items listed below are features of a democracy.

■ Every citizen has a say in how the country is run. (A **citizen** is a member of a community, such as a town, a state, or a nation.)

■ Every citizen can vote.

■ Citizens vote for their leaders.

■ Citizens go along with the vote of the majority.

Many countries are run as democracies today. The United States and Canada are two examples.

■ PRACTICE 3: Democracy

Circle the letter of the correct answer to each question below.

1. Which of the following is one thing a citizen CANNOT do in a democracy?
   a. have a say in government
   b. tell others what to do
   c. vote for their leaders
   d. go along with the majority

2. Which of the following describes a democracy?
   a. The people in city A do not vote.
   b. The people in city B do as they please. There are no leaders.
   c. The people in city C vote for their leaders.
   d. The people in city D do exactly what their leader says.

Monarchy

A local charity club called The Givers has been around for 20 years. The Winsure family has always run The Givers. Regina Winsure runs every meeting. She makes up all of the rules. Club members must adopt any new rules she decrees. Regina Winsure is training her oldest child to run The Givers one day.

The Givers is run like a *monarchy*.

The items listed below are features of a monarchy.

■ One person—the **monarch**—rules the country.

■ Most monarchs inherit power. This means that the power is passed down from one generation to the next.

■ The monarch (king, queen, emperor, empress) rules for life.

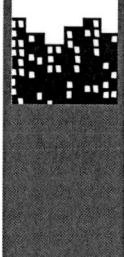

Most modern monarchs have no real power at all. In such cases, the monarch is not a real ruler. He or she is a living "symbol" of the country. But other people actually run the government. For example, you may have read about Queen Elizabeth II of England. England is part of the United Kingdom. The United Kingdom (England, Scotland, Wales, and Northern Ireland) is a **constitutional monarchy**. This means that Queen Elizabeth's main role is to represent the United Kingdom during state occasions and ceremonies. She is the "head of state." The queen does not, however, run the government. This is the job of the **prime minister.**

■ PRACTICE 4: Monarchy

Circle the letter of the correct answer to each question below.

1. What is a monarch?
    a. a citizen in a democracy
    b. a leader of a club
    c. someone who inherits power and rules for life
    d. a person voted into power

2. Which statement describes a monarchy?
    a. The ruler receives power for life by a vote of the people.
    b. The ruler inherits power for life after his or her parents' deaths.
    c. The ruler kills the monarch to get power for life.
    d. The ruler shares power with a dictator.

Dictatorship

Dean Saur is a member of the social committee at his workplace. One day he got sick and tired of listening to other social committee members. He took control of the committee. Members were afraid to stand up to Dean. Now they do what he says. He runs the social committee the way he wants.

Dean's social committee is run like a *dictatorship.*

The items listed below are features of a dictatorship.

- One person, the **dictator,** runs the country by force.

- The dictator has all the power.

- The dictator may try to control people's beliefs.

- People are not allowed to criticize the dictator.

There are a few other words that have about the same meaning as *dictatorship.*

They are

- **tyranny**

- **totalitarian state/totalitarianism**

- **despotism**

Other words also mean about the same as *dictator.*

They are

- **tyrant**

- **despot**

You may have seen the movie *Evita.* This movie focused on the life of Eva (or Evita) Perón, the wife of Juan Perón. Juan and Evita Perón ruled Argentina from 1946 to 1955. When Juan Perón ran for president, he used police and armed thugs to stop any opposition. Once he was president, he controlled the government through his army. The people of Argentina lost many rights and freedoms.

However, Juan and Evita also did many good things. They gave wage increases and better benefits to workers. They also established thousands of hospitals, schools, and orphanages. Do you think it is possible to have a "good" dictatorship? Would you be willing to give up your freedom in exchange for higher wages and better social programs? Write your answer on a separate sheet of paper.

■ PRACTICE 5: Dictatorship

Circle the letter of the correct answer to each question below.

1. What rights do citizens have in a dictatorship?
   a. They have no rights.
   b. They can vote.
   c. They can choose their leaders.
   d. They can do anything they please.

2. Which statement describes a dictatorship?
   a. The government can force people to pay any tax.
   b. The government cannot force people to pay taxes.
   c. There is no government at all.
   d. The people vote on whether or not to pay taxes.

3. Which word means about the same as *dictatorship*?
   a. monarchy
   b. democracy
   c. anarchy
   d. despotism

4. Which word means about the same as *dictator*?
   a. representative
   b. tyrant
   c. monarch
   d. anarchist

5. Draw a line from each name for a ruler to the name for a state. The words in each pair should have the same root, or basic part. The first one is done for you.

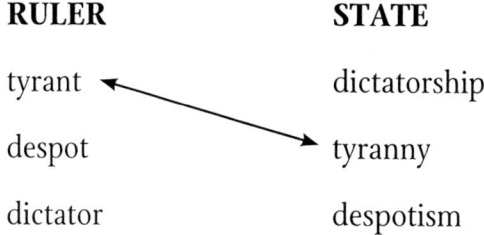

RULER   **STATE**

tyrant   dictatorship

despot   tyranny

dictator   despotism

LESSON 2: Moderate Versus Extreme Government

 GOAL: To learn to differentiate between democracies and dictatorships

WORDS TO KNOW

extreme   moderate

Extreme Ideas Versus Moderate Ideas

Just about any activity can be carried to an extreme. Consider the example of eating. It is an activity that most people enjoy. But eating everything in sight, day and night, is **extreme**. Eating too little, such as nothing but carrot sticks, is also extreme. Eating a reasonable amount, not too much or too little, is **moderate**. Moderate is in the middle.

Just about any idea can be carried to the extreme, too. For example:

Idea	Extreme
Fruit is good for you.	You eat nothing but fruit.
People need enough sleep.	You go to bed at 6 P.M. every night.

People's ideas about government can also be extreme or moderate. Some people have extreme ideas, such as those listed below.

- "I want absolutely no government at all."

- "I expect to control every part of citizens' lives."

- "I want all citizens to vote on every single issue."

Many people have moderate ideas about government, such as the ones that follow.

- "I want as little government as possible."

- "I want to control some parts of citizens' lives."

- "I want citizens or their representatives to vote on important issues."

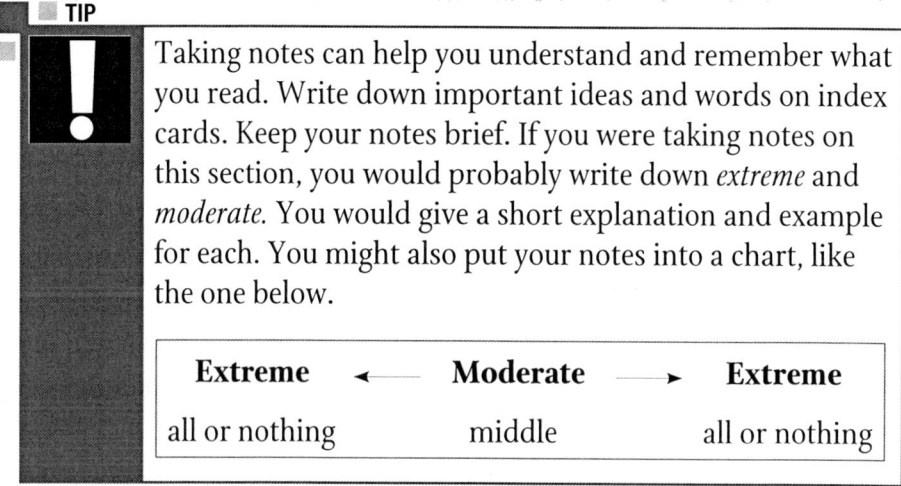

TIP

Taking notes can help you understand and remember what you read. Write down important ideas and words on index cards. Keep your notes brief. If you were taking notes on this section, you would probably write down *extreme* and *moderate*. You would give a short explanation and example for each. You might also put your notes into a chart, like the one below.

Extreme ◄———	**Moderate** ———►	**Extreme**
all or nothing	middle	all or nothing

■ PRACTICE 6: Extreme Ideas Versus Moderate Ideas

Write *extreme* or *moderate* to describe each statement below.

1. "One ruler should run this country. No one else should have any say."

   _____

2. "One ruler should decide important issues in this country. The citizens can make other decisions."

   _____

3. "People should vote whenever they can."

   _____

4. "People should never, ever miss a vote."

   _____

How Democracy Differs from Dictatorship

In many ways, democracy is the opposite of dictatorship. The chart below shows some of the differences.

Differences Between Democracy and Dictatorship

DEMOCRACY	DICTATORSHIP
Every citizen can vote.	Citizens cannot vote.
Every citizen has a say in how the country is run.	One ruler has all the say.
Citizens can vote to change their leaders.	Citizens cannot criticize their leader or vote to change leaders.
Citizens have rights.	Citizens have no rights.

IN REAL LIFE

In times of crisis, such as wartime, democracies may temporarily become more like dictatorships. Citizens may have some of their freedom taken away. One example of this was the internment of Japanese Americans during World War II. In February 1942, the U.S. government arrested 80,000 U.S. citizens living on the West Coast. These citizens were all of Japanese descent. They were forced to live in special camps away from the coast. They lost much of their property. The government defended this action as a wartime necessity. They feared Japanese Americans would aid Japan during the war. In fact, not one Japanese American was ever accused of being a spy during World War II.

The chart on the next page summarizes what you have learned about three forms of government. It also gives a few examples of each form of government in the world today.

Three Forms of Government

TYPE	HOW IT WORKS	COUNTRIES
Democracy	Citizens have a say; citizens vote, majority rules.	United States, Canada, Mexico, India, Italy
Monarchy	Monarch inherits rule; monarch rules for life; monarch may be just a symbol of power.	United Kingdom, Monaco
Dictatorship	One person takes all power; citizens have no rights.	China, Cuba, Vietnam, North Korea

■ PRACTICE 7: How Democracy Differs from Dictatorship

Use the chart above to answer the following questions.

1. Which form of government allows people to vote for their leaders?

   _____

2. Which form of government gives all of the power to one person?

   _____

3. Which form of government would most likely punish its citizens for criticizing the leader?

   _____

4. Which form of government would most likely protect its citizens from unfair punishment?

   _____

Look at the sample countries listed in the chart on page 13. For each form of government, choose a sample country that is familiar to you. Write what you already know about that country. This will help you remember what each form of government is about. For example, the United States is a democracy. Think about how the United States works. This will help you remember what a democracy is.

5. Democratic country _____

   What do you know about this democracy?

   _____

   _____

6. Monarchy _____

   What do you know about this monarchy?

   _____

   _____

7. Dictatorship _____

   What do you know about this dictatorship?

   _____

   _____

8. Now choose a country from each category that is unfamiliar to you. Research that country and write what you find out about the country.

   _____

   _____

   _____

   _____

   _____

   _____

LESSON 3: Forms of Democracy

GOAL: To understand the differences between direct democracy and representative democracy

WORDS TO KNOW

direct democracy   **representatives**

representative democracies

Now that you have learned about three major forms of government, you will focus on democracy. You will recall that democracy is a form of government in which authority rests with the people. In this lesson, you will learn about the two main forms of democracy: direct democracy and representative democracy.

Direct Democracy

A **direct democracy** usually refers to citizens making policy and law decisions in person. A direct democracy exists when all members of a group can vote on every issue. The New England town meeting is an example of direct democracy. Citizens of a community meet to vote directly on issues affecting the town. Here are some other examples of direct democracy.

- Every member of the neighborhood group can vote on what time the Fourth of July parade starts.

- Every member of the tennis team can vote on the color of the uniform.

- Every member of the school association can vote on how much money they will give for new books.

Direct democracy works well only when the group is not too large. It is not an efficient system for large groups. Direct democracy does not exist on a national level anywhere in the world today.

■ PRACTICE 8: Direct Democracy

Answer each of the following.

1. Circle the letter of each statement that shows a direct democracy.
   a. All residents in a city can vote for a mayor to run the city.
   b. All members of a work team can vote on the time of their lunch break.
   c. All members of a club can vote on which color uniform to order.
   d. All members of a bowling club can vote on where to have their tournament.

2. Why would direct democracy NOT work for the U.S. government? Explain.

   _____

   _____

   _____

Representative Democracy

As you just learned, direct democracy does not work well with large groups. It would be confusing to have a large number of people vote on every single issue. Instead, most democratic states and countries have **representative democracies.**

In a representative democracy, citizens vote for **representatives.** A representative is someone who acts in your name. For example, suppose you need to buy a radio but you are too sick to go to the store. What can you do? One idea might be to ask someone else to go for you. In other words, you would have another person *represent* you. That person would be your *representative.*

In government, each representative represents many people. Citizens choose their representatives by voting. These representatives will then make decisions for them. Before voting, citizens learn about the people who are running for office. They vote for the people who will best represent their ideas. The United States is a representative democracy.

That means that if you are a U.S. citizen, you should vote for your representatives. Your representatives make decisions for you.

In a representative democracy (such as the United States), citizens can also vote their representatives *out* of office. This may happen because of several things.

■ Citizens are unhappy with a decision one of their representatives has made.

■ They do not like the way one of their representatives is doing the job.

■ They want a change.

Here is a quick review of representative democracy.

■ Citizens vote for people who represent their ideas.

■ Each representative makes decisions for many citizens.

■ Citizens may vote their representatives out of office.

■ Representative democracy is efficient for large groups.

■ PRACTICE 9: Representative Democracy
Answer each of the following.

1. Circle the letter of each statement that describes a representative democracy.
    a. Members of a book club vote on how much to charge for dues.
    b. Members of an exercise club vote for a leader who will charge dues.
    c. Members of a union vote on a leader to decide whether to strike.
    d. Members of a union vote on whether to strike.

2. Is your state government a representative democracy? Explain.

_____

_____

_____

Representatives or Issues?

Your neighborhood group is taking some votes today. They are voting on

- who will attend the city planning meeting

- who will attend the local school board meeting

These are votes for *representatives.*

They are also voting on

- how much money to spend on recycling bins

- which park they should clean up first

These are votes on *issues.*

In a representative democracy, people vote both for representatives and on issues.

■ PRACTICE 10: Representatives or Issues?

Decide whether each vote below is for a representative or on an issue. Write *representative* or *issue* on the line.

1. You vote for someone who wants to lower taxes.

   _____

2. You vote for a law to lower taxes.

   _____

3. You vote against a five percent sales tax.

   _____

Two Kinds of Democracy

The diagram on page 19 shows how the two kinds of democracy are alike. It also shows how they are different.

How Are They Alike?

Direct Democracy   **Representative Democracy**

- Every citizen has a say in how the country is run.

- Every citizen can vote.

- Citizens go with the majority vote.

How Are They Different?

Direct Democracy   **Representative Democracy**

- Citizens vote on every issue.   - Citizens do not vote on every issue.

- Citizens do not vote for representatives.

- Citizens do vote for representatives.

- Representatives vote on many issues.

TIP

The chart above helps you understand direct democracy and representative democracy by comparing and contrasting them. *Comparing* helps you to see how the ideas are alike. *Contrasting* helps you to see how they are different. Using a chart or diagram can help you compare and contrast any two ideas.

On another sheet of paper, create a Venn diagram comparing and contrasting direct democracy and representative democracy. Notice how the diagram allows you to visualize, or "see," how the two concepts are alike and how they are different.

■ PRACTICE 11: Two Kinds of Democracy

Use the diagram on page 19 to answer each of the following.

1. Which statement shows a way in which the two kinds of democracy are alike? Circle the letter of the correct answer.
   a. Citizens can vote on every issue.
   b. Citizens vote for representatives.
   c. Citizens cannot vote on every issue.
   d. Citizens can vote.

2. Which of the following statements show a way in which direct democracy and representative democracy differ? Circle the letters of the correct answers.
   a. Citizens vote for representatives.
   b. Citizens can vote.
   c. Citizens go with the majority vote.
   d. Citizens vote on every issue.

3. Explain why the New England town meeting is an example of direct democracy.

   _____

   _____

   _____

   _____

   _____

THINK ABOUT IT

How much do you need to know about a person before you choose him or her as your representative? Today, journalists report on even the most private parts of politicians' lives. This is especially true during elections. You may often see newspaper or television reports of bad behavior, unusual personal habits, and more. Do you think this type of information is important? Where would you draw the line? Write your answer on a separate sheet of paper.

UNIT 1 REVIEW

Circle the letter of the correct answer to each of the following questions.

1. What type of government has no rules, no elections, and no laws?
    a. a democracy
    b. anarchy
    c. a monarchy
    d. a dictatorship

2. What is a country where one person inherits the power to rule?
    a. a democracy
    b. anarchy
    c. a monarchy
    d. a totalitarian state

3. What is a country where one person rules by force?
    a. a democracy
    b. anarchy
    c. a monarchy
    d. a totalitarian state

4. Which type of government does NOT have total power to rule the people?
    a. a democracy
    b. a dictatorship
    c. tyranny
    d. a totalitarian state

5. The leader of a revolution overthrows a country's elected representatives. The dictator becomes the only ruler of the country. What type of government is this?
    a. a democracy
    b. anarchy
    c. a monarchy
    d. a totalitarian state

6. Which of the following is an extreme statement?
   a. "I will vote whenever I can."
   b. "I will never vote again."
   c. "I do not agree with your decision."
   d. "I decided not to vote this year."

7. Which of the following is a moderate statement?
   a. "I do not always agree with your decisions."
   b. "I will never agree with your decisions."
   c. "I will always agree with your decisions."
   d. "I have decided never to listen to your decisions again."

8. What is a country where everyone votes on every decision?
   a. a direct democracy
   b. a monarchy
   c. a representative democracy
   d. a totalitarian state

9. What is a country where citizens vote for people who make the laws?
   a. a direct democracy
   b. a monarchy
   c. a representative democracy
   d. a totalitarian state

10. Under which system are citizens MOST responsible for the laws of their country?
   a. a direct democracy
   b. anarchy
   c. a monarchy
   d. a representative democracy

UNIT 1 APPLICATION ACTIVITY
Government in Your Own Life

In Lesson 1, you learned about three different forms of government: *democracy, monarchy,* and *dictatorship.* You also learned that the absence of any laws or rulers is called *anarchy.* One way to understand these forms of government is to look for signs of them in your own life. To do this, think about one of the groups you belong to. Some examples are families, households, community or church groups, sports teams, classes, clubs, or even groups of friends. Now, answer the questions about your group below.

Type of group:_____

Does this group have a leader? If so, who is it? _____

_____

How did this person become the group's leader? _____

_____

_____

What are the leader's responsibilities? _____

_____

_____

What are your responsibilities as a member of the group? _____

_____

_____

How are decisions made? _____

_____

How much of a say do you have in making decisions? Is everyone's opinion equally important? _____

_____

Now, think about which type of government plan your group follows. In the space below, write a brief paragraph. Tell which form of government your group represents, and explain why. (Look at Lesson 1, page 4, if you need to review the different forms of government.)

_____

_____

_____

_____

_____

_____

_____

_____

_____

_____

_____

_____

_____

_____

_____

UNIT 2
The Constitutional Framework

LESSON 4: Introduction to the U.S. Constitution

GOAL: To understand the historical context for the American independence movement and its founding documents

WORDS TO KNOW

Articles of Confederation

colonists

colony

Constitution

Continental Congress

Declaration of Independence

delegates

president

principles

What Is the Constitution?

The U.S. **Constitution** is a written document. It explains the rules for running the government of the United States. The Constitution has now been in force for over 200 years. This is longer than any other written constitution of any other nation. Although much has happened in our country, the Constitution has remained much the same. In over 200 years, there have only been 27 amendments to the Constitution.

The Constitution is the supreme law, the highest law of the land. No person in this country is free from following its rules. No part of the United States government is free from following its rules, either.

The Constitution did not spring up overnight. It grew out of the first Americans' fight for freedom. The Constitution is also the result of compromises worked out by the founders of our country.

Although the Constitution is our highest law, that does not mean it cannot be changed. The people who wrote our Constitution wanted to make it flexible. They wanted to make sure it would still make sense as society changed. So, rules within the Constitution allow for changes.

■ PRACTICE 12: What Is the Constitution?

Circle the letter of the correct answer to each question.

1. Which U.S. citizens are free from following the Constitution?
   a. wealthy citizens
   b. elderly citizens
   c. government workers
   d. none of the above

2. Circle the letter of the statement that is TRUE.
   a. The Constitution can be changed.
   b. The Constitution can never be changed.

3. How long has our current Constitution been in force?
   a. over 300 years
   b. less than 200 years
   c. over 200 years
   d. none of the above

4. Circle the letter of the statement that is FALSE.
   a. There have been no changes to the Constitution in over 200 years.
   b. The Constitution is our country's highest law.

TIP

You may come across words in this book that you do not know. When you see an unfamiliar word, look at the text around the word for *context clues*. Context clues can help you understand the meaning of a word you do not know. For example, the text on page 27 uses the word *supreme*. You may not know what this word means. Look at the sentence surrounding the word *supreme*. The phrase *highest law of the land* is used to describe the same thing as *supreme law*. This tells you that *supreme* probably means "highest."

The Declaration of Independence

In 1607, England settled its first colony in the "new world" of North America, at Jamestown. A **colony** is a group of people who live in a new territory but are still partly controlled by their home country. The colony at Jamestown did not last. The **colonists,** or people living in the colony, did not know how to provide for themselves in the new land. Also, there was a constant shortage of supplies from England. Still, by the late 1600s, England had settled 13 other colonies. Most of these colonies were in what is today the northeastern United States. The 13 colonies were the following:

Connecticut	New Hampshire	Rhode Island
Delaware	New Jersey	South Carolina
Georgia	New York	Virginia
Maryland	North Carolina	
Massachusetts	Pennsylvania	

On July 4, 1776, these 13 colonies declared their independence from England. The colonists were angry with England. They believed that the English government was ignoring their rights. They decided to form their own government.

The colonists wrote the **Declaration of Independence.** In this document, they argued for their right to form a new nation. They explained the wrongs done to the colonies by the English king. They stated that the 13 colonies were now an independent country.

The Declaration of Independence stated three basic **principles.** These beliefs served as the foundation of the United States government. The three basic principles of the Declaration of Independence are listed below.

- All people are created equal.

- All people have a right to life, liberty, and the pursuit of happiness.

- Government should carry out the wishes of the people.

■ PRACTICE 13: The Declaration of Independence

Circle the letter of the correct answer to each of the following questions.

1. Why did the colonists want to form their own government?
   a. They wanted to go back to England.
   b. They did not want too much power for themselves.
   c. They believed that England was ignoring their rights.
   d. They wanted to become part of Spain.

2. Which of the following is a basic principle of the Declaration of Independence? (*Hint:* There is more than one correct answer.)
   a. Government should carry out the wishes of the people.
   b. Government should provide clothing, shelter, and food for the people.
   c. All people are created equal.
   d. All people have a right to life, liberty, and the pursuit of happiness.

The Articles of Confederation

In 1777, **delegates,** or representatives, from the 13 colonies wrote the country's first constitution. This group of representatives was known as the **Continental Congress.** The constitution they wrote was called the **Articles of Confederation.**

The Continental Congress worried about giving their new government too much power. They did not want to trade the English king for another harsh ruler. So, the Articles of Confederation called for a weak national government.

In fact, the new government was too weak. At least 9 out of the 13 colonies had to agree on any law. It was rare for so many colonies to agree, so the government had trouble passing laws. The new government also had no **president,** so there was nobody in charge who could carry out the laws. And, the new government had no courts, so there was no way to settle disputes.

■ PRACTICE 14: The Articles of Confederation

Circle the letter of the correct answer to each of the following questions.

1. Under the Articles of Confederation, how many states had to agree on new laws?

    a. 13

    b. 9

    c. 10

    d. 8

2. Why did the new government have trouble carrying out laws?

    a. There was no president.

    b. There were no courts.

    c. It was too strong.

    d. There was no constitution.

3. Why did the new government have trouble settling disputes?

    a. There was no president.

    b. There were no courts.

    c. It was too strong.

    d. There was no constitution.

IN REAL LIFE

The act of writing a new constitution may seem like a page from history, but countries around the world are still writing new constitutions today. For example, Czechoslovakia had to write a new constitution when it broke free from the former Soviet Union in 1989. Then, in 1993, Czechoslovakia split into two countries: the Czech Republic and Slovakia. To prepare for this split, the Czech government had to write another new constitution, passed in December 1992.

LESSON 5: The Constitutional Convention of 1787

GOAL: To learn the historical context behind the Constitutional Convention and the major compromises involved in drafting the Constitution

WORDS TO KNOW

compromise

Congress

Constitutional Convention

Electoral College

electors

Executive Compromise

Great Compromise

House of Representatives

New Jersey Plan

regulate

Senate

Three-Fifths Compromise

Virginia Plan

Background on the Convention of 1787

The 13 colonies won the War of Independence from England, also called the American Revolution. In 1783, England recognized American independence in the Treaty of Paris. But, as the new American government took its first steps, it became clear that the Articles of Confederation were not working. The new government was not effective. In 1787, therefore, 55 delegates went to Philadelphia to revise the Articles of Confederation. All 13 states, except for Rhode Island, sent representatives. This large gathering was called the **Constitutional Convention.**

Each state had its own ideas about what the revised constitution should say. Northern states disagreed with southern states. Large states and small states had different opinions. So did rich states and poor states, merchant states and farming states, slave states and free states. In the end, the spirit of **compromise** won. Every state gave up something for the common good. Every state also received something it had wanted.

The Constitutional Convention lasted for a whole summer. The result of this meeting was the Constitution of the United States. It is basically the same document that runs our government today.

■ PRACTICE 15: Background on the Convention of 1787

Circle the letter of the correct answer to each of the following questions.

1. What was the original purpose of the Constitutional Convention?
   a. to declare war on England
   b. to write the Declaration of Independence
   c. to write the Articles of Confederation
   d. to revise the Articles of Confederation

2. Why was the convention able to succeed?
   a. The majority ruled.
   b. The large states tricked the smaller states.
   c. No state had to give up anything.
   d. Every state was willing to compromise.

The Great Compromise: Our Congress

The delegates at the Constitutional Convention debated many difficult issues. One of the most difficult questions was how states would be represented in the new national government.

States with many citizens, like Virginia, wanted representation based on state population. Their plan was called the **Virginia Plan.** This plan said that more populous states deserved to have more say in government.

Smaller, less populous states disagreed. They wanted each state to have an equal number of representatives. Their plan was called the **New Jersey Plan.** This plan said that each state should have an equal voice.

Delegates finally reached a solution. It was called the **Great Compromise.** The legislative (law-making) branch of government, or **Congress,** would have two parts, or houses. The **House of Representatives** would be based on population. But, in the **Senate,** each state would have exactly two representatives.

This compromise gave more representatives to the larger states. But, it gave smaller states power, too.

■ PRACTICE 16: The Great Compromise: Our Congress

Circle the letter of the correct answer to each of the following questions.

1. Which plan was passed during the Constitutional Convention?
    a. the Virginia Plan
    b. the New Jersey Plan
    c. the Great Compromise
    d. none of the above

2. What was the Great Compromise?
    a. a solution to the problem of representatives in Congress
    b. a plan presented by representatives from Virginia for a new Congress
    c. a plan presented by representatives from New Jersey for a new Congress
    d. a solution to the problem of British influence in the new government

TIP

Pay attention to cause and effect in your reading. A *cause* is an event that brings about another event, the *effect.* Most events are both a cause and an effect. For example, the colonists' belief that England was ignoring their rights (cause) led to the American Revolution (effect). The American Revolution (cause) led to the need to form a new government (effect). The need to form a new government (cause) led to the debate over representation (effect). The debate over representation (cause) led to the Great Compromise (effect), and so on. Paying attention to cause and effect can help you remember the sequence of events.

The Three-Fifths Compromise

A second problem facing the Constitutional Convention was slavery. Southern states believed that slavery was necessary to their way of life. But some northern states thought slavery was wrong. These states had made slavery illegal. Should slaves be included in the population count? Should Congress **regulate,** or have control over, the slave trade?

Southern states wanted slaves counted as part of the population. That would increase their population, which would allow them to send more representatives to Congress. But they did not want slaves counted for taxes, which would increase the amount they had to pay the national government. Northern states disagreed. They argued that if slaves were to be counted as part of the population, they should also be counted for taxation.

In the end, delegates settled on the **Three-Fifths Compromise.** They agreed that each slave would be counted as three fifths of a free man. This meant that three fifths of the slaves in a state would be counted for both population and taxation. Delegates also compromised on the slave trade. Congress, they agreed, would not try to regulate the trade in slaves for at least 20 years.

■ PRACTICE 17: The Three-Fifths Compromise

Circle the letter of the correct answer to each of the following questions.

1. How did southern states think slaves should be counted?
   a. as part of the population
   b. for tax purposes
   c. both *a* and *b*
   d. none of the above

2. What did the Three-Fifths Compromise state?
   a. that every free man would be counted as three fifths of one slave
   b. that every slave would be counted as three fifths of one free man
   c. that all slaves would be counted as full members of the population
   d. that all slaves would be counted like free men for tax purposes

The Executive Compromise

A third difficult issue facing delegates at the Constitutional Convention was what to do about a president. They worried about giving one person too much power. After all, the colonies had suffered under the King of England. But they also knew that they needed a strong leader. Without a strong leader, their new government would not work.

The delegates' solution was the **Executive Compromise**. The Executive Compromise called for a president, but it put limits on his or her power.

- The president's term would last only four years. After four years, the president would have to run for reelection if he or she wanted to stay in office.

- Congress was given the power to remove the president from office.

The delegates also worried about how to elect a president. They decided that citizens would not vote directly for president. Instead, they formed the **Electoral College,** which would be made up of representatives, called **electors.** Citizens would choose the electors. The electors would then choose the president in a meeting of the Electoral College.

■ PRACTICE 18: The Executive Compromise

Circle the letter of the correct answer to each of the following questions.

1. Which of the following was NOT stated in the Executive Compromise?
   a. The president's term will last only four years.
   b. Congress will have the power to remove the president from office.
   c. The president must have every decision approved by the vice president.
   d. all of the above

2. Why did the delegates at the Constitutional Convention worry about a president?
   a. They knew they needed a weak leader.
   b. They wanted a leader like the King of England.
   c. They didn't want one person having too much power.
   d. none of the above

3. What is the purpose of the Electoral College?
- **a.** to advise citizens on the best candidates
- **b.** to elect the president
- **c.** to elect senators
- **d.** to elect electors

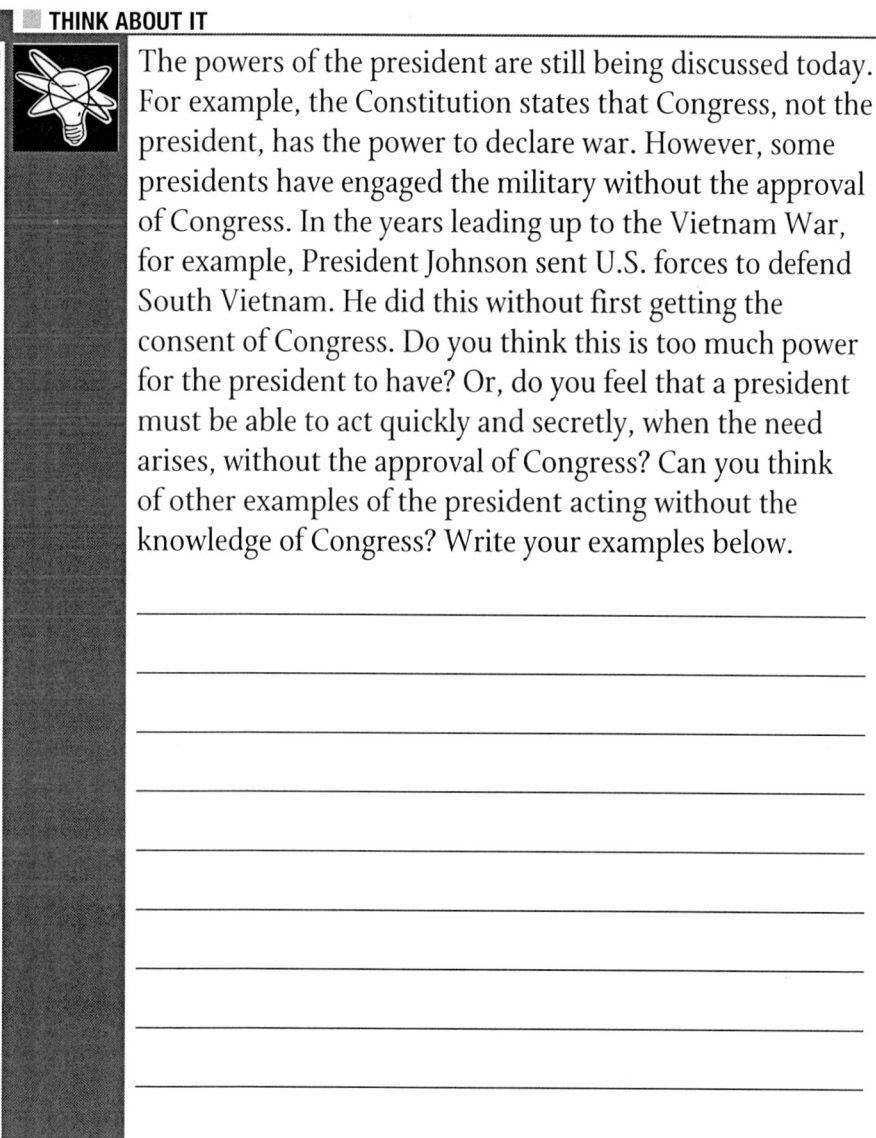

THINK ABOUT IT

The powers of the president are still being discussed today. For example, the Constitution states that Congress, not the president, has the power to declare war. However, some presidents have engaged the military without the approval of Congress. In the years leading up to the Vietnam War, for example, President Johnson sent U.S. forces to defend South Vietnam. He did this without first getting the consent of Congress. Do you think this is too much power for the president to have? Or, do you feel that a president must be able to act quickly and secretly, when the need arises, without the approval of Congress? Can you think of other examples of the president acting without the knowledge of Congress? Write your examples below.

_____

_____

_____

_____

_____

_____

_____

_____

_____

_____

LESSON 6: The Philosophy and Principles of the Constitution

GOAL: To understand the basic concepts of the United States' most important document of government

WORDS TO KNOW

checks and balances	judicial branch
executive branch	legislative branch
federalism	self-government
inherent rights	

Key Ideas in the Constitution

The basic philosophy, or way of thinking, of the Constitution is **federalism.** Under federalism, power is divided between our national government and state governments. By dividing power in this way, federalism ensures that the national government can meet the needs of the nation. At the same time, federalism allows for the strength and uniqueness of individual states.

Certain powers belong to both state and national governments. For example, the national government has the power to declare war and to set foreign policy. But state governments control education in their state. Some powers are shared. For example, federal and state governments both set taxes, borrow money, and build roads.

The most important principle in the Constitution is **self-government,** or government by the people. According to the Constitution, the people of the United States elect representatives. These representatives carry out the wishes of the people. Through their representatives, the people can make and change laws. They can even change the Constitution. If representatives don't follow the wishes of the people, the people can elect different representatives.

■ PRACTICE 19: Key Ideas in the Constitution

Circle the letter of the correct answer to each of the following questions.

1. What is federalism?
   a. the power of the national government
   b. the power of the state governments
   c. the division of power between national and state governments
   d. the limitations put on the power of the president

2. What does "government by the people" mean?
   a. that the citizens can control the government
   b. that each branch of the government has different powers
   c. that the states pay taxes to the federal government
   d. that the Constitution is the highest law of the land

Other Principles of the U.S. Constitution

There are also other important principles in the Constitution. The second main principle is that of **inherent rights.** This means that all people have a right to life, liberty, and the pursuit of happiness. *Inherent* means "primary" or "basic." Citizens do not have to do anything to get these rights. They are born with them. The principle of inherent rights was first stated in the Declaration of Independence. It is the basis for all rights listed in the Constitution, such as the right to a fair trial.

The third main principle of the Constitution is separation of powers. Our nation's founders did not want any one person or group of people to have too much power. So, they created a government with three branches, or parts. Each branch has certain powers, and it has *only* those powers. Together, the three branches run the government.

- ■ The **executive branch** carries out laws. The executive branch is headed by the president.

- ■ The **legislative branch,** or Congress, makes laws.

- ■ The **judicial branch** interprets laws. The judicial branch is headed by the Supreme Court.

■ PRACTICE 20: Other Principles of the U.S. Constitution

Circle the letter of the correct answer to each of the following questions.

1. What principle is the basis of all rights listed in the Constitution?
   a. federalism
   b. balance of powers
   c. inherent rights
   d. separation of powers

2. What does "separation of powers" mean?
   a. that all branches of government have the same duties
   b. that Congress is divided into two houses
   c. that every president must have a vice president
   d. that each branch of government has certain powers, and only those powers

Checks and Balances

The Constitution clearly defines the powers of each branch of government. It also sets up a system of **checks and balances.** This means that each branch has ways to check, or control, the other two branches. Each branch balances the power of the other two. No branch becomes too strong. No branch becomes too weak.

The three branches check and balance one another in several ways. Here are some examples.

- The Supreme Court can strike down a law passed by Congress by ruling that it is against the Constitution.

- The Supreme Court can stop an action taken by the president.

- The president can veto, or refuse to sign, a law passed by Congress. (The president must sign a law for it to go into effect.)

- Congress can override, or set aside, the president's veto.

- The president appoints, or chooses, Supreme Court justices.

- Congress can refuse to approve a president's choice of a Supreme Court justice.

The Checks and Balances System

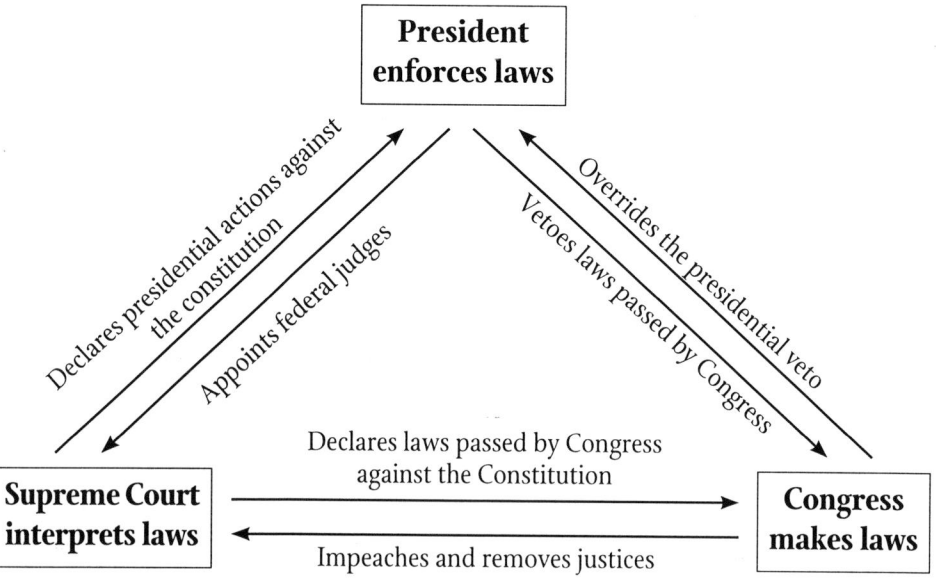

President
enforces laws

Declares presidential actions against the constitution

Appoints federal judges

Overrides the presidential veto

Vetoes laws passed by Congress

Supreme Court
interprets laws

Declares laws passed by Congress
against the Constitution

Impeaches and removes justices

Congress
makes laws

■ PRACTICE 21: Checks and Balances

Circle the letter of the correct answer to each of the following questions.

1. What is the purpose of checks and balances?
   a. to balance power between the two houses of Congress
   b. to stop any one branch of government from getting too much power
   c. to limit the president's term to only four years
   d. to give Congress the power to remove the president from office

2. How can Congress check the power of the president?
   a. by stopping the Supreme Court's actions
   b. by vetoing the president's laws
   c. by overriding, or setting aside, the president's veto
   d. by choosing Supreme Court justices

3. How can the Supreme Court check the power of Congress?
   a. by striking down a law passed by Congress
   b. by removing justices from the court
   c. by overriding the president's veto
   d. all of the above

LESSON 7: The Structure of the Constitution

 GOAL: To become familiar with the Preamble, articles, and amendments that make up the U.S. Constitution

WORDS TO KNOW

amendments	guarantee	ratify
articles	Preamble	
Bill of Rights	prohibited	

The Three Main Sections of the Constitution

The Constitution has three main parts: the Preamble, the articles, and the amendments.

- The **Preamble** is the introduction to the Constitution. It presents the philosophy of our government. It explains why the Constitution was written.

- The **articles** describe the setup and workings of the government.

- The **amendments** are new sections added to the Constitution over the years. The first ten amendments are called the **Bill of Rights.** They explain the basic rights of U.S. citizens.

The Preamble to the Constitution

We the People of the United States, in Order to form a more perfect Union, establish Justice, insure domestic Tranquility, provide for the common defence, promote the general Welfare, and secure the Blessings of Liberty to ourselves and our Posterity, do ordain and establish this Constitution for the United States of America.

Unit 2: The Constitutional Framework • American Government

As you read the Preamble to the Constitution, you may notice that some of the spelling and grammar looks wrong. Why was *Order* capitalized? Why did they spell *defence* with a *c*? First, remember that the colonists were from England. The spelling of many English words has changed over time in the United States. Even today, there are many words that are spelled differently in England and the United States. For example, Americans write *defense* while the English write *defence.* Americans write *center* while the English write *centre.* Also, back in the 1700s it was common to capitalize all nouns in a sentence. For example: *I went to the Store to buy Milk, Cheese, and Bread.*

■ PRACTICE 22: The Three Main Sections of the Constitution

Circle the letter of the correct answer to each of the following.

1. What do the articles of the Constitution describe?
   a. the amendments
   b. the structure and workings of government
   c. the inherent rights of citizens
   d. an introduction to the Constitution

2. New sections added to the Constitution are called _____.
   a. the Preamble
   b. amendments
   c. the Bill of Rights
   d. articles

The Articles

The Constitution has seven articles. They are the foundation of the United States government. They describe how the government is set up. The seven articles are listed in the box on page 44.

▪ **Article I**	sets up the legislative branch; lists the duties and powers of this branch
▪ **Article II**	sets up the executive branch; lists the duties and powers of this branch
▪ **Article III**	sets up the judicial branch; lists the duties and powers of this branch
▪ **Article IV**	sets up the relationship between national and state governments
▪ **Article V**	sets up the rules for changing the Constitution
▪ **Article VI**	sets up the Constitution as the highest law of the country
▪ **Article VII**	describes how the Constitution should be approved by the states

▪ PRACTICE 23: The Articles

Circle the letter of the correct answer to each of the following questions.

1. Which article sets up the Constitution as the highest law of the country?
    a. III
    b. V
    c. IV
    d. VI

2. Which article sets up the judicial branch?
    a. I
    b. III
    c. II
    d. IV

3. Which article sets up the executive branch?
   a. I
   b. III
   c. II
   d. IV

The Bill of Rights

Many delegates at the Constitutional Convention wanted the Constitution to protect people's rights. They wanted to give the people a **guarantee,** or promise, that these rights would never change. The delegates decided to address these rights in 10 amendments, or changes, to the Constitution. These amendments are known as the Bill of Rights. They explain the rights of all people living in the United States. The Bill of Rights includes the amendments listed in the box that follows.

First Amendment	protects freedom of speech and religion (the right to say, print, or think whatever you wish)
Second Amendment	protects the right to own and carry guns
Third Amendment	protects people from having to shelter soldiers in their homes against their wishes
Fourth Amendment	protects people from "unreasonable searches" by the government (requires the government to have a reason to search)
Fifth Amendment	protects the right to "due process of law"; protects people from being tried for the same crime twice in the same court; protects people from being forced to be witnesses against themselves; protects people from being denied life, liberty, or property without proper legal proceedings.
Sixth Amendment	protects a person's right to a fair trial
	(continued on next page)

(continued from previous page)	
Seventh Amendment	protects the right to have a trial by jury
Eighth Amendment	protects people from cruel or unusual punishments if found guilty of a crime
Ninth Amendment	protects individual rights not actually listed in the Constitution
Tenth Amendment	protects states' rights

■ PRACTICE 24: The Bill of Rights

Circle the letter of the correct answer to each of the following questions.

1. How many amendments are in the Bill of Rights?
   a. four
   b. nine
   c. seven
   d. ten

2. Which amendment protects people from an unreasonable search of their home?
   a. first
   b. second
   c. third
   d. fourth

3. Which amendment protects your right to a fair trial?
   a. fifth
   b. sixth
   c. seventh
   d. eighth

4. Which amendment protects other rights not listed in the Constitution?
   a. sixth
   b. seventh
   c. eighth
   d. ninth

TIP

The Bill of Rights is the heart of the U.S. Constitution. You have just read a short outline of what each amendment in the Bill of Rights contains. You may also want to read a copy of the actual amendments. This will give you the full description of your rights. Plus, you will be able to read the amendments in their original language. You can find a copy of the Constitution and Bill of Rights in any edition of *The World Almanac.* You can also find it on the Internet at http://www.house.gov. This site provides links to the Constitution, amendments to the Constitution, and the Declaration of Independence. The Bill of Rights is included in an appendix at the back of the book.

Amending the Constitution

The founders of our country wanted the Constitution to be flexible. As the country changed, the Constitution might also need to be changed. But they did not want it to be too easy to change the Constitution.

There are two steps to changing, or *amending,* the Constitution.

Step 1. Congress has to propose an amendment. To do this, two thirds of Congress must vote to support the amendment. Congress can also propose an amendment by holding a special convention, called by two thirds of the states. This second method has never been used.

Step 2. After Congress proposes an amendment, the states have to **ratify,** or accept, the amendment within seven years. At least three fourths of the states must ratify the amendment for it to become part of the Constitution.

Over 200 years have passed since the states ratified the Constitution and Bill of Rights. Since then, only 17 additional amendments have been ratified.

■ PRACTICE 25: Amending the Constitution

Circle the letter of the correct answer to each of the following questions.

1. How many members of Congress must support an amendment for it to pass?
   a. two thirds of the members
   b. three quarters of the members
   c. at least half of the members
   d. all of the members

2. What is the last step in amending the Constitution?
   a. Congress proposes an amendment.
   b. At least two thirds of Congress support the amendment.
   c. At least three quarters of the states ratify the amendment.
   d. Congress holds a special convention, which is called by the states.

3. How much time do the states have to ratify an amendment proposed by Congress?
   a. seven years
   b. three years
   c. six years
   d. four years

Other Amendments

As you know, the first 10 amendments of the Constitution are the Bill of Rights. They guarantee our basic rights. There have been 17 other amendments to the Constitution. Some of these amendments are listed below. The year following each amendment is the date it was ratified, or approved, by the states. As you just learned, that is the last step in making an amendment part of the Constitution.

■ **Amendment 13** (1865) made slavery illegal.

■ **Amendment 15** (1870) gave all men the right to vote, regardless of race or color.

- **Amendment 16** (1913) gave Congress the right to tax the money people earn (income tax).

- **Amendment 19** (1920) gave women the right to vote.

- **Amendment 20** (1951) states that no person can be elected president for more than two terms.

- **Amendment 24** (1964) **prohibited** voting taxes (made them illegal).

- **Amendment 26** (1971) lowered the voting age to 18 years.

■ PRACTICE 26: Other Amendments

Circle the letter of the correct answer to each of the following questions.

1. Which amendment gave Congress the right to tax people's income?
   a. Amendment 12
   b. Amendment 16
   c. Amendment 15
   d. Amendment 19

2. Which amendment made slavery illegal?
   a. Amendment 13
   b. Amendment 15
   c. Amendment 19
   d. Amendment 26

3. In what year were women given the right to vote?
   a. 1865
   b. 1889
   c. 1901
   d. 1920

4. Which amendment limited the president to two terms in office?
   a. Amendment 15
   b. Amendment 20
   c. Amendment 24
   d. none of the above

Have you ever heard of the Equal Rights Amendment, also known as the ERA? This amendment was first introduced in Congress in 1923. It was just after ratification of the 19th Amendment, which gave women the right to vote. The ERA was mainly designed to end unfair practices against women. Its main principle was that men and women must be given the same legal rights. It took 49 years for Congress to pass the ERA. It finally passed in 1972. The ERA was then sent to the states to be ratified. Within the first year, it had been ratified by 30 states. It needed only eight more states to become law. But even with a three-year extension, the ERA could not gain the necessary majority. People against the ERA argued that it would take away special protections for women, such as alimony and child support. They argued that if the ERA passed, women would be drafted into the military, just like men. In 1982, the ERA failed. However, supporters of the ERA continue to try to pass the amendment. They have introduced it in every session of Congress since 1982.

Making Government Work

The U.S. Constitution set up a government *by the people.* This means that citizens have a voice in government. For this type of government to work, citizens must also have duties. For example, citizens should obey the laws other citizens have helped to form. Citizens should also learn about the issues and events happening around them. They should let a representative know if they are happy or unhappy with his or her work. They can do this by writing letters. They can also do this with their vote.

Voting is an important way for citizens to take a stand. Citizens can vote for representatives who have ideas close to their own. They can work for candidates they like. Or, they can work to defeat candidates.

Representatives have responsibilities, too. It is their job to work for voters and other government officials. It is their job to protect the Bill of Rights. It is their job to look after the best interests of the nation. A good representative balances the country's interests with the interests of the people he or she represents.

Working together, citizens and representatives keep our government strong.

■ PRACTICE 27: Making Government Work

Circle the letter of the correct answer to each of the following questions.

1. Which of the following is NOT a duty of U.S. citizens?
    a. overriding the president's veto
    b. obeying laws
    c. staying informed
    d. voting

2. Which of the following is NOT a duty of representatives?
    a. working for voters
    b. balancing local and national interests
    c. acting alone, without the influence of citizens
    d. protecting the Bill of Rights

UNIT 2 REVIEW

Circle the letter of the correct answer to each of the following questions.

1. Which is an important principle of the Constitution?
    a. separation of powers
    b. government by the people
    c. inherent rights
    d. all of the above

2. What does the Constitution describe?
    a. national government
    b. state governments
    c. local governments
    d. county governments

3. What is "separation of powers"?
   a. Each branch of government has a different area of control.
   b. Congress is divided into the Senate and the House of Representatives.
   c. The branches of government share all powers and duties.
   d. Power is divided between large and small states.

4. What does "government by the people" mean?
   a. that states pay taxes to the federal government
   b. that citizens control government with their votes
   c. that each branch of government has different powers
   d. that the president must be a U.S. citizen

5. What do the articles of the Constitution explain?
   a. the inherent rights of U.S. citizens
   b. the structure of national government
   c. changes to the Constitution
   d. the purpose of the Constitution

6. Which part of the Constitution lists the reasons why it was written?
   a. the Preamble
   b. the articles
   c. the amendments
   d. the Bill of Rights

7. How many amendments are there to the Constitution?
   a. 7
   b. 10
   c. 27
   d. 36

8. Which part of the Constitution contains guarantees of specific freedoms?
   a. the Preamble
   b. the articles
   c. the Bill of Rights
   d. the introduction

9. What does the system of checks and balances do?
   a. keeps each branch of government from getting too much power
   b. makes sure the three branches of government never work together
   c. gives the three branches of government exactly the same duties
   d. allows each branch of government to run the country on its own

10. What is the main function of the legislative branch?
   a. to explain laws
   b. to enforce laws
   c. to pass laws
   d. to interpret laws

UNIT 2 APPLICATION ACTIVITY
In Your Own Words

The U.S. Constitution was written in 1789. The English language has changed greatly since then. There may be some words in the Constitution that you have never heard before. Some of these words may not be used anymore. Others may just be more formal than the types of words you are used to.

Three voting amendments are copied below and on page 54, as they appear in the Constitution. Read each amendment. Then, rewrite each amendment using your own words. If you do not know the meaning of a word, look it up in a dictionary.

Amendment 15: The right of citizens of the United States to vote shall not be denied or abridged by the United States or by any State on account of race, color, or previous condition of servitude.

_____

_____

_____

_____

_____

_____

Amendment 24: The right of citizens of the United States to vote in any primary or other election for President or Vice President, for electors for President or Vice President, or for Senator or Representative in Congress, shall not be denied or abridged by the United States or any State by reason of failure to pay any poll tax or other tax.

_____

_____

_____

_____

_____

Amendment 26: The right of citizens of the United States, who are eighteen years of age or older, to vote shall not be denied or abridged by the United States or by any State on account of age.

_____

_____

_____

_____

_____

_____

UNIT 3

Political Parties and Voting

LESSON 8: Political Parties

GOAL: To learn about different types of political parties and their functions

WORDS TO KNOW

candidate	political party
coalition	primary elections
Democratic Party	Republican Party
general election	two-party system
independents	voting bloc

Parties and Their Candidates

Suppose you are shopping for a pair of boots. How do you choose?

- Look at one pair and take it.

- Let the clerk decide for you.

- Try on at least two pairs before deciding.

Most people prefer to try on at least two pairs. This way, they will have more than one pair from which to choose. They will have a better chance of buying a pair they like.

In a representative democracy, people have a choice. They choose between two or more political parties. A **political party** is a group that stands for certain ideas. The United States has two large political parties and several smaller ones. Other representative democracies in the world may have several strong parties and many weaker ones.

Most candidates join a political party. A **candidate** is a person running for a political office, such as senator or president of the United States. Being a member of a political party helps a candidate show voters how he or she stands on different issues.

Different political parties have different ideas about the following:

■ how the government should be run

■ how much power the government should have

■ how money should be spent

■ how much tax money to collect from citizens

■ how to protect citizens' rights

■ PRACTICE 28: Parties and Their Candidates

Write the answer to each question below.

1. What is a political party?

_____

_____

2. How many political parties do representative democracies have?

_____

_____

3. What is a political candidate?

_____

_____

4. What are some issues on which a political candidate might have specific views?

_____

_____

_____

5. Name three offices for which a political candidate might run.

_____

_____

_____

The Two-Party System

The United States has a **two-party system.** This means that our country has two large political parties. They are the **Republican Party** and the **Democratic Party.** There are also many minor parties. These parties are much smaller and have less power than the two major parties. Some minor parties are the Socialist Party, the Green Party, and the Reform Party.

Americans differ widely in their opinions. But most voters support one major party or the other. They vote for the party with the ideas closest to their own.

THINK ABOUT IT

Many Americans think that the United States needs a third major political party. They feel as though neither the Democratic Party nor the Republican Party represents what they believe in. Others think that a third party will only weaken one major party or the other. In the 2000 election, Ralph Nader ran for president as a Green Party candidate. He received less than 3 percent of the nationwide vote. But some believe that he took enough votes away from Al Gore, the Democratic candidate, that Gore lost the election. What do you think?

When U.S. citizens register to vote, they may join a political party. This allows them to vote in that party's **primary elections.** A primary election is when members of a party choose a candidate for president. The candidates from each party then run against one another in a **general election.**

Some voters do not join any party. They are called **independents.** In many states, independent voters may not vote for party candidates in primary elections. In other states, independent voters may vote for primary candidates, but they may only vote in either the Democratic or

Republican primary, not both. They choose a party and, after voting, they can return to being independent before they leave the place of voting by declaring so. All independents may vote in general elections.

■ PRACTICE 29: The Two-Party System

Answer each of the following.

1. Check all of the following statements that are TRUE.
   - ☐ **a.** Independents cannot vote in general elections.
   - ☐ **b.** Independents often cannot vote in primary elections.
   - ☐ **c.** The United States has many major parties.
   - ☐ **d.** The United States has two major parties.

2. What is a primary election? _____

   _____

3. Why can independent voters NOT vote in primary elections in many states?

   _____

   _____

Governments with Many Parties

Some representative democracies have six or more major political parties. This may seem like too many parties. How does one party get enough votes to win an election or pass a law? In some cases, several parties agree to vote together. They form a **voting bloc**, or **coalition**. This means that they join together to have more power. A coalition may run a government for a long time, or it may last a short time.

Voting blocs can also happen in the United States. Remember, the United States has only two major parties. However, there can be any number of minor parties. Sometimes, representatives from the same party do not agree. There may be a group of representatives who agree with another party's ideas. They may form a voting bloc with the other party. One of the larger parties may also ask smaller parties for support. In this way, both parties increase their own power.

■ PRACTICE 30: Governments with Many Parties

Write the answer to each question below on the lines provided.

1. How do laws get passed in countries with many parties?

   _____

   _____

2. How many minor parties could the United States have?

   _____

   _____

Governments with One Party

Some totalitarian governments have only one party. The government and the party are the same. The party runs the government.

Citizens may even vote in such one-party systems. In fact, they may get into trouble if they do not vote. But these citizens have no choice.

In a one-party system, the government decides who runs for office. The government makes sure that its candidates support the "party line." This means they must support the ideas of the party and of the government. In that way, the government makes sure it stays in power.

IN REAL LIFE

For some people, May Day (May 1) is a day for celebrating springtime. For people who lived in the former Soviet Union, though, May Day was a very different sort of holiday. The Communist Party ruled the political, economic, social, and cultural life of the Soviet people for much of the twentieth century. During this time, May Day was made an official holiday. Soviets had to participate in parades to show their support for the government. Those who did not participate risked being punished. For many Soviets, May Day was a day of fear and oppression.

■ PRACTICE 31: Governments with One Party

Answer each of the following.

1. Circle the letter of the correct answer. A one-party system is a
    _____.
    a. representative democracy
    b. direct democracy
    c. dictatorship
    d. monarchy

2. In a one-party system, who decides who the candidates will be?

    _____

Different Party Systems

The chart below reviews what you have just learned about different party systems. It also lists examples of countries with each type of system.

System	Number of Parties/ Candidates	How It Works	Countries
one party	one or none	Government chooses candidates, or no elections.	Cuba, China
two party	two major ones	Citizens vote for representatives of two major parties.	United States, Canada
many parties	several small ones	Citizens vote. Parties form coalitions.	Italy, Israel

◼ PRACTICE 32: Different Party Systems

Use the chart on page 62 to answer each question below. Write your answer on the lines provided.

1. How many candidates does a system with one party have?_____

2. Which countries have one-party systems?

   _____

3. Which countries have two major parties? _____

   _____

4. How does a system with many parties work? _____

   _____

5. How many candidates does a system with many parties have?

   _____

   _____

6. What are two countries that have systems with many parties?

   _____

   _____

7. Can you name the leader of a country with a one-party system?

   _____

   _____

8. Do you think that having only one political point of view would be an advantage or a disadvantage? Explain.

   _____

   _____

   _____

   _____

LESSON 9: Power and Our National Government

 GOAL: To explore the concepts of large versus small government and the stability of different forms of government

WORDS TO KNOW

federal budget   **stable government**   **stalemate**

The Size of Government

In a representative democracy like the United States, political parties take stands on issues that affect our everyday lives. Look in the newspaper. You can probably find a story that tells about a party's actions or plans.

One of the most basic issues that political parties debate is the size and power of the government. Many people talk in words of "big" versus "small" government. How much power should the government have? How should the government use its power?

- to build housing for poor people?

- to stop unions from striking?

- to make businesses charge fair prices?

- to protect the environment?

Look at the diagram below. This diagram represents the kind of debate you have just read about. Where do you stand?

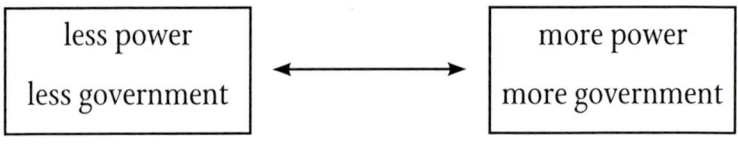

| less power | | more power |
| less government | ⟷ | more government |

Now look at the situations that follow. Each situation asks whether or not government should get involved. This will help you find out where you stand on the issue of "small" versus "big" government. It will also show you how complex the issue can be. This is why political parties are still debating it today.

> **Situation 1:** A trucking union goes on strike. No one is delivering food. There may be a food shortage.
>
> **Question:** What should the government do?

If you want the government to have more power

The government should force the union and the trucking companies to work out an agreement. The country cannot risk a food shortage.

If you want the government to have less power

The government should not do anything. Let the union and the trucking companies resolve the situation themselves.

> **Situation 2:** A drug company owns the rights to a new medicine that will save many lives. Since they own the rights, no one else can make this medicine.
>
> **Question:** Should the government make sure that the drug company charges a fair price?

If you want the government to have more power

The government should set a price for the medicine. People must have access to it at a fair price.

If you want the government to have less power

The government should not have any say over the price. The price should be set by the marketplace.

Political parties debate issues like these every day. Sometimes, political parties need to compromise to keep government running smoothly. This is when the people on each side of an issue get *some* of what they want. Each side also has to give up some of what it wants. Nobody is completely happy. But nobody is completely unhappy, either. If the parties on each side refuse to compromise, they may reach a **stalemate**. This is when nothing gets done.

IN REAL LIFE

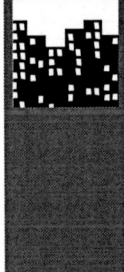

When stalemates happen in government, they can have dramatic effects. One such stalemate happened in December 1995. At this time, the U.S. House of Representatives was led by Republicans. The U.S. President, Bill Clinton, was a Democrat. The two sides could not agree on a federal budget. The **federal budget** is the plan for all the money the U.S. government receives and spends. Without a federal budget, the government could no longer pay its employees or keep its organizations open. The government had to shut down. This shutdown lasted for 21 days. Some 280,000 government workers went without pay. The stalemate ended on January 6, 1996. It was the longest shutdown in U.S. government history.

■ PRACTICE 33: The Size of Government

Answer each of the following.

1. Check each statement that shows a compromise.
   - ☐ **a.** "We will strike until we get what we want from the company."
   - ☐ **b.** "The company will never give in to any of the union's demands."
   - ☐ **c.** "The union will end the strike. The company will raise salaries over a few years."
   - ☐ **d.** "The company will charge whatever it wants for the medicine."
   - ☐ **e.** "The company will go along with a reasonable price determined by a private study."
   - ☐ **f.** "The government will tell the company exactly what it can charge for the medicine."

2. Check which of the following represents "small" government.

- [ ] **a.** The government steps in to settle a strike.
- [ ] **b.** The government passes a law that requires companies to offer childcare services for its workers.
- [ ] **c.** The government sets up a social welfare program for single mothers.
- [ ] **d.** The government lets each individual business decide whether or not it will offer health insurance for its workers.

TIP

! Look at the term *primary elections.* The word *primary* can help you understand what this term means. *Primary* means "first." Primary elections always happen first, before the general elections. You can also think of the word *primer.* When you are painting a room, you put a coat of *primer* on the walls first. Then you put the paint on top of the primer.

Stable Government

Today, two-party government systems tend to be very stable. A **stable government** is orderly. Its work gets done. Laws get passed. Laws are enforced. Taxes get collected. People's rights are protected. Most citizens are satisfied.

Here are features of a stable government.

- It is orderly.

- Work gets done.

- Citizens are satisfied.

But what happens when a government changes every few months or years? That sometimes happens with governments with more than two parties. It also happens a great deal with dictatorships. Such a government is not stable. Its work does not get done. The people may suffer. The result may be anarchy—no government at all.

■ PRACTICE 34: Stable Government

Circle the letter of the correct answer to each question below.

1. Some modern countries are ruled by military dictatorships. These governments do not tend to be stable. They usually last for only a few months or years before another group takes power from them. This can happen again and again. What kind of government might result?
   a. anarchy
   b. direct democracy
   c. monarchy
   d. representative democracy

2. Why do the United States and Canada have stable democracies?
   a. They are governed by a president and vice president.
   b. They have only a few major political parties.
   c. They have many major political parties.
   d. They have large populations.

■ IN REAL LIFE

Many areas of the world remain unstable. One example is the country of Somalia. For most of the 1990s, Somalia was in a state of anarchy. In 1991, a civil war forced Somalia's dictator to flee. By 1992, the United Nations declared Somalia to be a country without a government. Six years later, in 1998, there was still no effective government. Instead, there were as many as 12 family "clans" fighting for power. There were no reliable laws or social organizations. The civil war, drought, and widespread crime were devastating for the Somali people. By 2004, the country had areas of stability. But most of the country still remains under the control of fighting factions.

LESSON 10: What Is the Democratic Process?

GOAL: To learn about the rights and duties of citizens in a democracy

WORDS TO KNOW

democratic process   eligible to vote

How to Make Democracy Work

In a democracy, voters listen to different opinions. They consider different sides of each issue. Then they vote. Citizens go along with the results of the vote or election. Voters may disagree with the party that wins. Yet they cooperate anyway. The country runs smoothly, even though citizens have different opinions. Everyone in a democracy can express his or her ideas. It does not matter whether the majority agrees or not. This is the **democratic process.** The democratic process can only work when the conditions listed below occur.

- Citizens vote.
- All citizens are allowed to express their opinions.
- Most citizens hold moderate views.
- Citizens cooperate with the majority.
- Representatives support citizens' interests.

■ PRACTICE 35: How to Make Democracy Work

Check each statement that is TRUE of citizens in a democracy.

- ☐ **1.** Most citizens hold extreme views.
- ☐ **2.** Citizens can have different opinions.
- ☐ **3.** Citizens do not cooperate with the government.
- ☐ **4.** Most citizens cooperate with the majority.

Democracy and Voting

Suppose your neighborhood group has a problem. Most of its members missed the last meeting. Only a few members voted.

- They voted on a new recycling project.

- They voted for a new leader.

- They voted to charge the other members dues.

The group members who did not vote are now angry. They do not like the new project. They do not agree with the new leader. And they say they will not pay the new dues. What went wrong?

In a democracy, every citizen has a responsibility to vote. If citizens do not vote, the democracy will not work.

■ PRACTICE 36: Democracy and Voting

Answer each of the following below.

1. Check all of the following statements that are TRUE.

   ☐ **a.** Citizens who do not vote will not get to choose their leader.

   ☐ **b.** Citizens who do not vote may be unhappy with the results.

   ☐ **c.** Citizens who do not vote will not have a say about their taxes.

   ☐ **d.** If no citizens vote, democracy will work anyway.

2. Why is it important to vote? Write your answer below.

   _____

   _____

The Voting Amendments

The United States has been a democracy from the start. However, many people did not always have the right to vote.

When slavery was allowed, slaves could not vote. For a long time, women could not vote. Some states had laws that kept poor people from voting. Some states had laws that kept other groups from voting. These laws lasted for many years.

Over time, the laws of the United States have changed so that more and more people could vote. You have learned that the Constitution is the highest law of our country, and that changes to the Constitution are called amendments. The chart below tells about the amendments that have let more people vote.

Date	Amendment	Change
1870	Amendment 15	gave voting rights to former slaves
1920	Amendment 19	gave voting rights to women
1964	Amendment 24	gave people the right to vote without paying a voting tax
1971	Amendment 26	gave voting rights to all citizens 18 years of age and older

 **IN REAL LIFE**

Women were not able to vote in this country until 1920. Many women worked hard to get the right to vote. They formed political groups that produced pamphlets and newsletters. They marched in protest and took part in hunger strikes. Many of them were jailed because of their protests. The right to vote is also called *suffrage,* and the women who fought for the right to vote are referred to as *suffragettes.* (Many men also worked hard so that women would have the right to vote, but this term doesn't apply to them.) Using reference material or the Internet, find information on a suffragette. On another sheet of paper, write a short biography of the woman you chose.

■ PRACTICE 37: The Voting Amendments

Write the answer to each question on the line provided.

1. What is at least one group of people who did NOT have the right to vote in the United States in 1865?

   _____

2. Which amendment helped poor people get the right to vote?

   _____

3. Which group got the right to vote first, women or former slaves?

   _____

Being Eligible to Vote

So, who gets to vote today?

In the United States, any citizen 18 years of age or older is eligible to vote. **Eligible to vote** means "allowed to vote."

The current laws of the United States protect the right of all citizens to vote. The factors listed below do *not* affect the right of U.S. citizens to vote.

- their race

- their sex

- their religion

- their ideas

- how much money they earn

- their lack of property

- their job

- their parents' nationality

■ PRACTICE 38: Being Eligible to Vote

Answer each question below.

1. Each person below is an American citizen. Check each person who can vote.

   ☐ **a.** a 23-year-old African-American man

   ☐ **b.** a 15-year-old Caucasian girl

   ☐ **c.** a 30-year-old Buddhist woman

   ☐ **d.** a 20-year-old Hispanic media intern

2. Did you check every person above? If not, explain why the person (or people) cannot vote.

   _____

   _____

   _____

   _____

3. The 26th Amendment was added to the Constitution in 1971. The amendment set the minimum age for voting in any election at 18 years of age. Before this amendment was adopted, the age requirement for voting was 21. At what age do you think citizens should be allowed to vote? Explain.

   _____

   _____

   _____

   _____

   _____

   _____

   _____

   _____

   _____

LESSON 11: Being a Responsible Voter

GOAL: To understand the need for voters to stay informed, evaluate facts and opinions, and vote regularly

WORDS TO KNOW

facts	opinions	register to vote

Citizens and Voting

What happens if there is an election and nobody comes?

Representative democracy works *only if citizens vote.* Nobody can make a U.S. citizen vote. But voting is everyone's duty as a citizen.

In the 2000 U.S. presidential election, there were approximately 205 million people of voting age. However, only about 51 percent of those eligible to vote did in fact cast a ballot. This means that more than 100 million people could have voted but did not.

It is important not only to vote, but to vote responsibly. What does this mean? A responsible voter should do the following:

- learn about his or her government

- learn about the people running for office

- understand the different sides of the issues

- vote regularly

If a voter does not understand the issues, he or she cannot make an intelligent decision when voting. Remember, every vote counts! You want to make sure that your vote is for the side with which you truly agree. Learn about issues in your community, city, state, and country. Read the newspaper; watch the news on television. If you can, go to a variety of news sources for information. Try to stay informed on a daily basis so that you are not overwhelmed with information at election time.

■ PRACTICE 39: Citizens and Voting

Check each statement that shows a responsible voter.

☐ **1.** "I listen only to people who agree with me."

☐ **2.** "I vote for the person who is the best dresser."

☐ **3.** "Once I make up my mind, I never change it."

☐ **4.** "I try to understand your opinion, even though I might disagree."

☐ **5.** "I read about different issues in the newspaper."

☐ **6.** "I never vote for anybody over 50 years old."

THINK ABOUT IT

You have just learned that a responsible voter researches information about issues and candidates before voting. However, most people do not have much free time. How could you start learning more about the issues in your community, state, and country? What is a realistic goal for yourself? Write your answer on a separate sheet of paper.

Voter Registration

Suppose you are running for town council. But most people in your town do not vote. What might you do to help your chances of winning?

Get your neighbors, friends, and supporters to sign up. Have them **register to vote** at City Hall. Citizens cannot vote if they have not filled out the correct forms in advance. This is state law.

Voter registration helps to keep the voting system honest and fair. It stops people from voting more than once in the same election.

Every registered voter is assigned a place to go to on election day. The voting place depends on the voter's address. This is the only place where he or she may vote.

Each voter must first check in at the voting place. His or her name is checked off a list. After this, the person enters the voting booth and votes. That person cannot vote again in the same election.

■ PRACTICE 40: Voter Registration

Write the answer to each question on the line provided.

1. What is an important reason for voter registration?

   _____

   _____

2. Why might voter registration stop some people from voting?

   _____

   _____

Weighing Facts and Opinions

When you vote, you make a decision about an issue or a candidate. How do you make decisions like these?

Before making any decisions, it is important to get information. Each issue will have many different sides. Voters should become familiar with each side before making up their minds.

When gathering information about an issue, be careful to separate facts from opinions. **Facts** are statements that can be proved. **Opinions** cannot be proved. For example, look at the statements below.

> *Thousands of people die in car accidents each year.*

This is a *fact*. It can be proved with statistics

> *The best way to keep people from dying in car accidents is to pass a seat-belt law.*

This is an *opinion*. It cannot be proved.

Pay attention to facts. They will help you understand an issue. But be careful about accepting other people's opinions as facts. They may not be true.

Suppose you have to vote on whether to keep voter registration in your state. How will you decide? The chart below shows some facts and opinions on this issue.

Issue: Should the United States keep voter registration?	
Fact 1: It requires time to register.	**Opinion 1:** It is a bother to register.
Fact 2: Registration makes it harder to cheat.	**Opinion 2:** Most people are too honest to cheat.
Fact 3: Less than half of eligible voters do vote.	**Opinion 3:** Citizens should be fined if they do not vote.
Fact 4: Registration of voters shows who can vote.	**Opinion 4:** Registration of voters is not necessary.

■ PRACTICE 41: Weighing Facts and Opinions

Label each statement that follows as *fact* or *opinion.*

1. Making people register to vote is government interference.

   _____

2. Less than half of all eligible voters vote. _____

3. The United States is a representative democracy. _____

4. This race for mayor is our most important election ever.

   _____

5. You can learn something about your state representative by reading the newspaper.

   _____

Why All Citizens Do Not Vote

Voting is a right. It is also a responsibility. However, there is no law to make people vote. Many Americans choose not to use this right.

Why do you think more citizens do not vote? Some believe that voter registration is too much trouble. They say that the government should make it easier to register.

Others believe that there are deeper reasons why people do not vote. Here are some possible explanations.

- Some Americans may feel out of touch with their representatives.

- Some Americans may feel their representatives do not work for them.

- Some Americans may believe that wealthy people have more influence.

■ PRACTICE 42: Why All Citizens Do Not Vote

Answer each question below.

1. Which of these statements is a fact? Circle the letter of the correct answer.
   a. Representatives are not in touch with their voters.
   b. American justice favors wealthy people.
   c. Voting is a right.
   d. Voter registration is a bother.

2. Why might being out of touch with their representatives keep people from voting? Write your answer on the lines provided.

   _____

   _____

THINK ABOUT IT

Statistics show that poorer people are less likely to vote than wealthier people. Why do you think this is so? Write your answer on a separate sheet of paper.

TIP

Certain key words can show you that a statement is an opinion, not a fact. Words such as *believe, feel,* and *think* signal that someone is stating a personal belief or opinion. Also, watch out for extreme words like *always* and *never.* People tend to use these words freely when stating opinions. They are used less frequently with facts.

UNIT 3 REVIEW

Circle the letter of the correct answer to each of the following questions.

1. What is the term for an organization that stands for certain ideas and policies?
   a. policy
   b. political party
   c. representative democracy
   d. two-party system

2. Which type of party system does the United States have?
   a. a one-party system
   b. a two-party system
   c. many parties
   d. anarchy

3. How many minor parties can there be in the United States?
   a. two
   b. five
   c. none
   d. any number

4. Which is usually the most stable form of government?
   a. a two-party system
   b. a six-party system
   c. a ten-party system
   d. a twenty-party system

5. Which kind of government would most likely have a one-party system?
   a. a representative democracy
   b. a direct democracy
   c. a dictatorship
   d. none of the above

6. What is a group of parties that band together for more power?
   a. a democracy
   b. a two-party system
   c. a one-party system
   d. a coalition

7. Which of the following is NOT true of citizens in the United States?
   a. Citizens can vote regardless of their race.
   b. Citizens can vote regardless of their sex.
   c. Citizens can vote regardless of their age.
   d. Citizens can vote regardless of their religion.

8. What does voter registration prevent citizens from doing?
   a. voting for state representatives
   b. voting twice in the same election
   c. voting in national elections
   d. voting for an independent party candidate

9. Which of the following is a fact?
   a. Senator Terry always listens to the people she represents.
   b. Senator Terry is out of touch with the voters.
   c. Senator Terry is aggressive and pushy.
   d. Senator Terry voted to lower taxes last year.

10. A citizen is trying to decide whether or not to vote for a new bottle-recycling plan. The citizen listens carefully to several speakers. The citizen reads about the issue in the paper. Then the citizen votes. When the results are announced, the citizen abides by the vote. This is an example of what?

    a. representative democracy
    b. the two-party system
    c. a primary election
    d. the democratic process

UNIT 3 APPLICATION ACTIVITY
The Importance of Voting

How important do you think voting is? In the space below, write a paragraph that describes your own thoughts about voting. If you are 18 years old or older, do you vote? Why or why not? If you are not old enough to vote yet, will you vote when you are of voting age? Why or why not?

_____

_____

_____

_____

_____

_____

_____

_____

_____

_____

_____

UNIT 4

The Federal Government

LESSON 12: What Is the Federal Government?

GOAL: To understand the three branches of the federal government and their functions

WORDS TO KNOW

branch of government   federal government

The Government and Its Divisions

The federal government is the national government. The **federal government** manages, or runs, the country. This is a huge job. About 5 million people work for the federal government. Postal workers, astronauts, and diplomats are federal employees. So are army, navy, and air force workers.

As set up in the Constitution, the federal government of the United States is divided into three parts, or branches:

- the executive branch

- the legislative branch

- the judicial branch

Each **branch of government** has certain duties.

- The legislative branch passes, or makes, laws.

- The executive branch carries out laws.

- The judicial branch interprets, or explains, laws.

Together, these branches run the government.

Washington, D.C., is the capital, or center, of the federal government. This is where the most important work of the government is done. Congress is in Washington, D.C. So is the Supreme Court. The White House (the home of the president) is also there.

■ PRACTICE 43: The Government and Its Divisions

Answer each of the following.

1. What is the federal government? Circle the letter of the correct answer.
   a. the state government
   b. the local government
   c. the national government
   d. the city government of Washington, D.C.

2. Where is the center of the federal government?

   _____

   _____

3. When a law is passed, it is *enacted*. Which branch of government is in charge of enacting laws?

   _____

   _____

4. What is the main duty of the executive branch? Circle the letter of the correct answer.
   a. to make laws
   b. to carry out laws
   c. to interpret laws
   d. to explain laws

TIP

The word *judicial* may be new to you. Here is an easy way to remember what it means: Think of the word *judge*. You are probably already familiar with this word. Notice how *judge* and *judicial* are similar. Both start with *jud-*. This is because both words come from the Latin word *judicare*. Try to remember the connection between *judge* and *judicial*. This will help you remember which branch of the government is the *judicial* branch.

LESSON 13: Separation of Powers

GOAL: To review the importance of the balance of power in a democracy

WORDS TO KNOW
separation of powers

Separation of Powers

The founders of our country divided the government into three parts. They did this so that no one person, or group of people, would get too much power. By dividing the duties of government, they divided its power.

The division of power into three parts is called the **separation of powers.** Together, the three branches share the power of government. Each branch has certain duties and powers. No one branch grows too strong. No one branch grows too weak. As a result, no one person can get too much power. No group of people can get too much power, either. This is very important to the American idea of democracy. Democracy is a form of government based on the belief that power should not belong to only one person or group of people.

■ PRACTICE 44: Separation of Powers
Answer each of the following.

1. What is the separation of powers? Write your answer below.

   _____

   _____

2. Why did the people who planned the U.S. government want separation of powers? Circle the letter of the correct answer.
   a. to make laws
   b. to be sure that no one person had too much power
   c. to carry out laws
   d. to be sure the new government was accepted by other nations of the world

LESSON 14: The U.S. Congress

WORDS TO KNOW

bicameral legislature	**recommend**
bill	**senator**
chamber	**session**
elect	**vetoes**
overrides	

Two Houses of Congress

Congress is the legislative branch of the federal government. Congress makes laws. These laws apply to the whole country. Congress is divided into two houses, or parts. A legislature with two parts is called a **bicameral legislature.** The two houses of Congress are the Senate and the House of Representatives.

The two houses of Congress meet for two-year terms. Each term begins on January 3rd of odd-numbered years. For example, the 109th Congress began in 2005 and ends in 2007. Congress meets in the Capitol Building in Washington, D.C. Each house has a **chamber,** or room, there. The period of time when Congress meets is called a **session.** In times of national emergencies, the president may also call a special session of Congress.

■ PRACTICE 45: Two Houses of Congress

Circle the letter of the correct answer to each of the following questions.

1. Which of the following is a house of Congress? (*Hint*: There is more than one correct answer.)
    a. the Senate
    b. the bicameral legislature
    c. the House of Representatives
    d. the chamber

2. What is a bicameral legislature?
    a. a legislature with a House of Representatives
    b. a legislature with a Senate
    c. a legislature with two parts
    d. any legislature

■ TIP

Look at the word *bicameral*. This word may be new to you. But if you break it apart, it will be easy to understand. The prefix *bi-* means "two." This prefix is used in many words you already know, such as *bicycle*. The root *camera* means "room" or "chamber." So, *bicameral* means "having two rooms or chambers."

The Senate and the House of Representatives

Both the Senate and the House of Representatives meet in the Capitol Building in Washington, D.C. These two houses of Congress make laws for the whole country. But each house is different.

The Senate is smaller than the House of Representatives. It has 100 members. These members are called **senators.** The people of each state in the United States get to **elect,** or choose, two senators to Congress. Every state has the same number of senators. Senators serve for terms of six years.

The House of Representatives is the larger house. Members of the House of Representatives are called *representatives*. The people of different states elect different numbers of representatives. Representatives serve for terms of two years. The number depends on each state's population. A state with many people has more representatives in Congress. A state with fewer people has fewer representatives in Congress. For example, in 2004 there were 53 representatives from California, 13 from Georgia, and only 1 from Delaware. At that time, the total number of representatives was 435.

■ PRACTICE 46: The Senate and the House of Representatives

Write the answer to each question on the line provided.

1. How many senators does each state send to Congress?

   _____

2. How many representatives does each state send to Congress? Explain.

   _____

   _____

   _____

THINK ABOUT IT

Who are the senators from your state? How many representatives from your state are in Congress? Would it be better to have more representatives from your state in Congress, or fewer? Why? Write your answer on a separate sheet of paper.

The Duties of Congress

The Constitution spells out the duties of Congress. But the powers of Congress are limited by separation of powers and checks and balances. The Senate and the House of Representatives share certain duties. Each house also has its own special duties.

The House of Representatives	The Senate
■ Introduces bills about budget or taxes ■ Impeaches (accuses) government officials of crimes	■ Confirms presidential appointments ■ Ratifies (approves) treaties with other governments ■ Determines whether government officials are innocent
Both Houses	
■ Control the money supply and making of money (paper and coins) ■ Borrow money from the government ■ Collect taxes ■ Control trade ■ Keep up the armed forces ■ Declare war ■ Control post offices across the country	

■ PRACTICE 47: The Duties of Congress

Circle the letter of the correct answer to each of the following questions.

1. What can the House of Representatives do that the Senate cannot?
    a. control trade
    b. confirm presidential appointments
    c. declare war
    d. impeach officials

2. What can the Senate do that the House of Representatives cannot?
    a. control trade
    b. confirm presidential appointments
    c. declare war
    d. impeach officials

How a Bill Becomes a Law: First Steps

Suppose you want a national law for punishing drunk drivers. How could this happen? First, a proposal would have to be written. A proposed law is called a **bill**. Once a bill is written, there are many steps to getting it passed into law.

Step 1: A senator or representative introduces the bill to Congress.

Step 2: A Senate or House committee studies the bill. The committee may or may not decide to **recommend**, or agree to pursue, your bill.

Step 3: If the committee recommends the bill, it is sent back to the Senate or House where it was first introduced. There, the bill is debated. Then there is a vote. The bill may be passed or defeated.

At steps 2 or 3, the bill might be changed. Even if it is not changed, it still has a long way to go.

■ PRACTICE 48: How a Bill Becomes a Law: First Steps

Circle the letter of the correct answer to each of the following questions.

1. Who can introduce a bill in Congress?
   a. only United States citizens
   b. only senators
   c. only representatives
   d. only members of Congress

2. What happens after a Senate or House committee recommends a bill?
   a. The bill is sent back to the Senate or House.
   b. A proposal is written.
   c. The bill gets introduced to Congress.
   d. The bill is studied by a committee.

How a Bill Becomes Law: Last Steps

Suppose your bill has passed the first three steps. In other words, the Senate or the House of Representatives has passed your bill. What happens next?

> **Step 4:** If your bill has been passed in one house, it is sent to the other house. There, it is debated. Again, your bill may be passed, defeated, or changed. If it is changed, it goes back to the first house.
>
> **Step 5:** If both houses agree on the bill and pass it, it goes to the president. If the president signs the bill, it becomes law. If the president **vetoes** (says no to) the bill, it does not become law.

If the president vetoes the bill, it can still become law. This can only happen if Congress **overrides,** or puts aside, the veto. To do this, two thirds of both houses must support the override.

The process of passing a law is long and complicated. Here is a flowchart to help you remember each step.

How a Bill Becomes a Law

> **INTRODUCTION OF A BILL**
>
> A senator or representative proposes a bill. The bill goes to a committee of the Senate or the House of Representatives.

↓

> **A COMMITTEE ACTS ON THE BILL**
>
> A committee studies the bill. If the committee recommends the bill, it goes back to the house where it started.
>
> *(continued on next page)*

↓

(continued)

CONGRESS ACTS ON THE BILL

A house of Congress debates the bill. If that house passes the bill, the bill goes to the other house. The second house of Congress debates the bill. If that house passes the bill, then both houses (Senate and House of Representatives) have to agree on any changes made to the bill.

PASSAGE OF THE BILL

The president must sign the bill for it to become law.

■ PRACTICE 49: How a Bill Becomes a Law: Last Steps

Circle the letter of the correct answer to each of the following questions.

1. What happens after one house of Congress passes a bill?
   a. It becomes law.
   b. It goes to the president.
   c. It is sent to the other house.
   d. It is changed.

2. What happens if both houses agree on a bill?
   a. It goes back to the first house.
   b. It goes to the president for his or her signature.
   c. It is sent to a committee for debate.
   d. It is rewritten.

3. How can Congress override a presidential veto?
   a. Congress sends the bill to a special committee.
   b. Congress revises the bill and sends it to the president.
   c. Congress supports the override by a two-thirds vote.
   d. none of the above

LESSON 15: The Executive Branch

GOAL: To learn about the key duties of the president and his or her administration

WORDS TO KNOW

Administration	enforces	secretary
Cabinet	independent agencies	vice president

What Is the Executive Branch?

The executive branch of the federal government **enforces,** or carries out, laws. The president, **vice president,** and special departments and agencies make up the executive branch. In the early days of our country, presidents had little staff. Today, however, the president's White House office has many aides and assistants who make up the president's closest staff.

The president is the top officer of the United States. He or she is the leader of the country and also serves as the commander in chief of the armed forces. In order for a person to become president, he or she must meet these requirements:

■ be a U.S. citizen born in the United States

■ be at least 35 years old

■ have lived in the United States for at least 14 years

The president's home is the White House in Washington, D.C. The president also has offices in the Capitol Building, where Congress meets. Members of the executive branch are also known as the **Administration.** To *administer* means to "direct or manage." The executive branch directs and manages our country. It keeps our country running smoothly.

■ PRACTICE 50: What Is the Executive Branch?

Circle the letter of the correct answer to each of the following questions.

1. Which executive officer leads the whole nation?
    a. the president
    b. the vice president
    c. Congress
    d. the senator

2. Which of the following is NOT a requirement for becoming president?
    a. to have at least four years of college
    b. to be at least 35 years old
    c. to have lived in the United States for at least 14 years
    d. to be a U.S. citizen born in the United States

3. What is the chief responsibility of the executive branch?
    a. It decides arguments about the meanings of laws.
    b. It enforces the laws of the land.
    c. It establishes all the laws of the land.
    d. none of the above

The President

The president has many responsibilities. The president's most important duties include the following:

■ enforcing the laws of the United States

■ carrying out foreign policy and maintaining relations with other countries

■ serving as head of the armed forces

■ approving or vetoing bills of Congress

■ advising Congress

■ making appointments of Cabinet members and to important federal jobs

You might think that the president would earn a very high salary, since he or she holds the highest office in the land. Actually, the president's salary is not very high when compared with the amount of responsibility that comes with the job. This is because the president is a public official whose salary is paid by the public (through taxes). In 2001, Congress approved a salary of $400,000 per year for the president. This might seem like a lot of money. But the presidents of most small and medium-sized companies in the United States earn 2, 5, or even 10 times as much! Do you think that the president should earn a higher salary? Why or why not? Write your answer on a separate sheet of paper.

■ PRACTICE 51: The President

Check each item below that states a duty of the president of the United States.

☐ **1.** enforcing laws

☐ **2.** approving bills passed by Congress

☐ **3.** making laws

☐ **4.** collecting taxes

☐ **5.** appointing people to federal jobs

☐ **6.** heading the armed forces

☐ **7.** advising Congress

The Vice President

The vice president is our nation's number two officer. Should anything happen to the president, the vice president would take over as president. The vice president has many duties. The most important duties include those listed on the next page.

- serving as president if the president cannot serve

- breaking any ties in the Senate

- acting as a link between the president and the Senate

- taking part in Cabinet meetings

- serving on the National Security Council

No other major government has an officer who compares to the vice president. In most other countries, a new election would be held immediately if a president died or had to leave office. In the United States, however, presidential elections are held only once every four years. This never changes, no matter how many times the office of president becomes open between elections. If a president dies or leaves office, the vice president takes over. If the vice president also dies or leaves office, the Speaker of the House of Representatives becomes president.

■ PRACTICE 52: The Vice President

Check each item below that states a duty of the vice president of the United States.

☐ **1.** serving on the National Security Council

☐ **2.** passing laws

☐ **3.** breaking ties in the Senate

☐ **4.** communicating with the president about the Senate

☐ **5.** collecting taxes

☐ **6.** heading the armed forces

The Cabinet

The **Cabinet** advises the president. Its members carry out his or her policies. Today the Cabinet is made up of the heads of 15 executive branch departments. Each department head is called a **secretary**. Each department has specific work to do. Here is a list of the 15 departments and their main areas of responsibility. They are listed in order of which secretary would first be chosen to act as president if other top officials could not.

Department	Main Concern
Department of State	foreign affairs
Department of the Treasury	money, taxes
Department of Defense	military matters, national safety
Department of Justice	legal matters
Department of the Interior	conservation, natural resources
Department of Agriculture	problems of farmers
Department of Commerce	business matters
Department of Labor	workers' issues and problems
Department of Health and Human Services	health and welfare
Department of Housing and Urban Development	housing programs
Department of Transportation	transportation
Department of Energy	energy policy and planning
Department of Education	education
Department of Veterans' Affairs	problems of those who have served in the U.S. armed forces
Department of Homeland Security	fighting terrorism against the United States

■ PRACTICE 53: The Cabinet

On the line provided, write the department to which each duty belongs.

1. Directing the army, air force, and navy

   _____

2. Protecting rivers from pollution

   _____

3. Making sure employers do not discriminate

   _____

Independent Agencies

The executive branch also includes many **independent agencies.** Here is a list of some important agencies and their main duties.

Agency	Main Job
National Aeronautics and Space Administration (NASA)	ensuring the peaceful use of space
Federal Deposit Insurance Corporation (FDIC)	insuring money deposited in banks
U.S. Commission on Civil Rights	preventing discrimination
National Science Foundation (NSF)	providing research grants for science
Federal Trade Commission (FTC)	keeping competition in business fair
Consumer Product Safety Commission	protecting consumers from unsafe products
Federal Communications Commission (FCC)	licensing television and radio stations, controlling telephone rates
Environmental Protection Agency (EPA)	setting standards for clean air and water; organizing pollution cleanups

■ PRACTICE 54: Independent Agencies

Circle the letter of the correct answer to each of the following questions.

1. Which agency is in charge of the space program?
   a. FDIC
   b. EPA
   c. NASA
   d. FTC

2. Which agency is in charge of keeping the rivers clean?
   a. FDIC
   b. EPA
   c. NASA
   d. FTC

3. Which agency is in charge of preventing discrimination in the workplace?
   a. the U.S. Commission on Civil Rights
   b. the Consumer Products Safety Commission
   c. the National Science Foundation
   d. the Environmental Protection Agency

IN REAL LIFE

You may not think that you have much contact with federal agencies in your day-to-day life. For example, how often would you need to speak with NASA? But, even though you may not realize it, government agencies are a part of your life. The money you deposit in your savings account is insured by the FDIC. The radio station you listen to on your way to work or school is regulated by the FCC. And, every piece of mail you send or receive is handled by the U.S. Postal Service. These are just some examples of how government agencies affect your everyday lives.

LESSON 16: The Judicial Branch

 GOAL: To learn about the basic structure and function of the U.S. court system

WORDS TO KNOW

appeal	due process of law
case	interprets
circuit courts	justices
civil case	plaintiff
constitutional/unconstitutional	precedent
criminal case	prosecutor
defendant	Supreme Court
district courts	verdict

Main Duties of the Judicial Branch

The judicial branch of the federal government **interprets** laws. This means that members of this branch make the meaning of laws clear. The judicial branch also explains the meaning of the Constitution, the law of the land.

As well as interpreting laws, the judicial branch settles disputes between the following:

- different states

- citizens of different states

- states and the federal government

- citizens and the federal government

- states and foreign governments

Finally, the federal courts swear in foreign-born people as citizens of the United States.

The top court in the judicial branch is the **Supreme Court.** Its rulings are final. All states and all people living in this country must follow the decisions of the Supreme Court.

Here is an example of how the judicial branch interprets laws:

Decades ago, Congress made a law requiring equal education for all children. Some states wanted separate public schools for black and white children. They said that their schools were "separate but equal." The Supreme Court had to decide what Congress's law meant by "equal" education. The court decided that separate schools were not equal. So, states had to allow both black and white children to attend the same public schools.

■ PRACTICE 55: Main Duties of the Judicial Branch

Circle the letter of the correct answer to each of the following questions.

1. Which type of dispute would the Supreme Court probably NOT settle?
   a. between one state and another state
   b. between a citizen and the federal government
   c. between a state and a foreign government
   d. between two citizens of the same state

2. Who does NOT have to follow a ruling of the Supreme Court?
   a. a citizen who has just moved to another state
   b. a foreigner living in this country
   c. a state that does not agree with the ruling
   d. none of the above

3. The Supreme Court is part of which branch of government?
   a. executive
   b. legislative
   c. judicial
   d. Congress

4. What is the main responsibility of the judicial branch?
   a. to make the laws
   b. to enforce the laws
   c. to interpret the laws
   d. to carry out the laws

5. What does it mean to "interpret" a law?
   a. to write a new law
   b. to make the meaning of a law clear
   c. to enforce a law

Structure of the Courts

The federal courts have different levels. As you know, the Supreme Court is the highest court in the country. All other courts are below the Supreme Court.

The **circuit courts** are the second-highest courts. They are a step below the Supreme Court. There are 13 circuit courts in the United States. The lowest-level federal courts are the **district courts**. There are 94 district courts. Most federal cases are first tried in district courts.

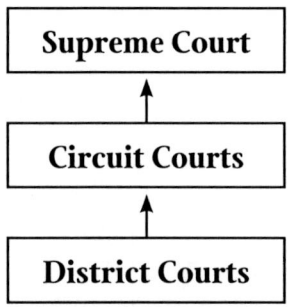

If a person is not happy with the decision of a district or circuit court, he or she can **appeal** the case to a higher court. This means that the person can request a new trial and hope to get the original decision overturned. A case can be appealed more than once, each time in a higher court. However, if the case reaches the Supreme Court, the decision will be final. Decisions of the Supreme Court cannot be appealed.

■ PRACTICE 56: Structure of the Courts

Circle the letter of the correct answer to each of the following questions.

1. How many Supreme Courts are there?
   a. 1
   b. 2
   c. 11
   d. 97

2. Where are most federal cases first tried?
   a. the Supreme Court
   b. district courts
   c. circuit courts
   d. Congress

Court Cases

A court **case** is an action in court. There are two kinds of court cases: criminal and civil. (See the chart below.)

Breaking a law may lead to a **criminal case.** For example, a murder could lead to a criminal case. So could burglary or arson (setting a fire on purpose). In a criminal case, the government accuses someone else of committing a crime. The government is the **prosecutor.** The person being accused is the **defendant.**

A dispute, or disagreement, may lead to a **civil case.** For example, a property dispute could lead to a civil case. So could an accident or a business disagreement. In a civil case, the person who brings the case to court is called the **plaintiff.** The person being accused is the defendant.

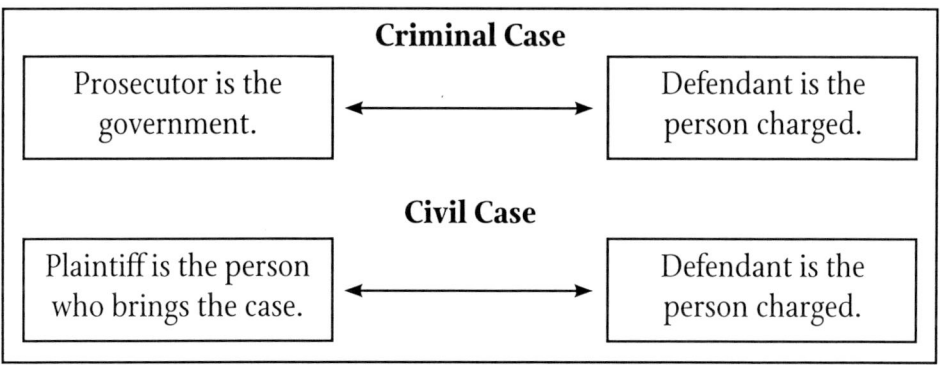

Criminal Case

Prosecutor is the government.	←→	Defendant is the person charged.

Civil Case

Plaintiff is the person who brings the case.	←→	Defendant is the person charged.

■ PRACTICE 57: Court Cases

Check each event below that could lead to a criminal case.

☐ **1.** Expensive jewelry is shoplifted from a store.

☐ **2.** There is a disagreement over who owns a winning lottery ticket.

☐ **3.** There is a dispute about where one neighbor's property ends.

☐ **4.** A disagreement leads to a murder.

☐ **5.** A restaurant is burned down for insurance money.

☐ **6.** People disagree about paying for an accident.

Citizens' Rights

The U.S. justice system assumes that a person is innocent until proved guilty. Everyone is guaranteed **due process of law.** This means that the government must follow the same fair rules in every criminal case. Every person has a right to a trial by jury. Every person has a right to remain silent. Every person has the right to call witnesses. Every person has the right to a lawyer.

A fair trial includes the right to appeal. An appeal involves asking that a **verdict,** or decision, be overturned. People often appeal a decision that they believe is unfair. An appeal may lead to a new trial. Or, prosecutors may decide not to try a case again.

■ PRACTICE 58: Citizens' Rights

Circle the letter of the correct answer to each of the following questions.

1. What is "due process of law"?
    a. overturning a verdict
    b. following fair rules in a trial
    c. committing a crime
    d. going without punishment

2. What does it mean to "appeal" a verdict?
   a. to request that a verdict be overturned
   b. to ignore the verdict of a court
   c. to take your case to a lower court
   d. to request that a verdict be explained

THINK ABOUT IT

In 1995, the criminal trial of O.J. Simpson attracted worldwide attention. O.J. Simpson, a former professional football star, was accused of murdering his former wife and her friend. The jury found that Simpson was not guilty of the crimes. In Lesson 7, page 45, you learned that the Fifth Amendment protects people from being tried for the same crime twice in the same court. Yet, in 1996, O.J. Simpson was taken to court again for the same murders in a civil trial. He was found guilty. How do you think this could happen? Write your answer on a separate sheet of paper.

The Supreme Court

The U.S. Constitution calls for a Supreme Court. It is the highest court in the land. The Supreme Court meets in Washington, D.C. Nine judges, called **justices,** sit on the Supreme Court. The Chief Justice acts as the leader of the court. Justices serve for life. When a justice dies or leaves the court for any reason, the president appoints a new justice. The Senate must approve each justice appointed by the president.

What happens when the Supreme Court decides to hear a case? First, the justices study similar cases from the past. They look for a precedent. A **precedent** is a decision made by past justices that can be applied to the case at hand. Finally, the justices vote. The majority decides the ruling. Often, a justice will write an opinion about a decision. It may be a majority opinion or a minority opinion. The majority opinion explains the legal thinking behind the ruling. The minority opinion explains the legal thinking of those who do not agree with the ruling. A Supreme Court decision is final and cannot be appealed.

■ PRACTICE 59: The Supreme Court

Circle the letter of the correct answer to each of the following questions.

1. How long may a justice keep his or her position?
   a. for 4 years
   b. for 10 years
   c. for as long as the president who appointed him or her stays in office
   d. for life

2. What can a plaintiff do if he or she does not agree with a Supreme Court ruling?
   a. appeal the ruling
   b. ignore the ruling
   c. send the ruling to Congress
   d. none of the above

Constitutionality

One of the jobs of the judicial branch is to interpret the Constitution. The Constitution is the highest law in the land. It protects the rights of American citizens. If people pass a law that conflicts with the Constitution, the judicial branch can decide that the law cannot be a law. In other words, the law might be **unconstitutional.** When people pass a law that agrees with the Constitution, it is **constitutional.**

For example, one of the rights protected by the Constitution is the right to free speech. Suppose a hate group has planned a march in your town to promote their ideas. Your town does not agree with this group's ideas. The town passes a law to keep the group from marching. According to the Constitution, members of the hate group can take your town to court. In time, the case could go to the Supreme Court.

The Supreme Court might decide that your town cannot stop a group from marching just because the town does not like the group's ideas. The Supreme Court might say that your town is interfering with the group's freedom of speech. In other words, your town's law might be unconstitutional.

Freedom of speech is one of the most basic rights protected in the Constitution. There are, however, certain limits on this freedom. One type of "speech" that has been controversial has been flag burning. In 1990, Congress passed a law making it illegal to burn American flags. Later that year, the Supreme Court ruled that this law was unconstitutional. The court said that the law went against a citizen's right to free speech, as protected in the Constitution. How do you feel about this issue? Write your answer on a separate sheet of paper.

■ PRACTICE 60: Constitutionality

Circle the letter of the correct answer to each of the following questions.

1. What is the highest law in the United States?

    a. laws passed by Congress

    b. the U.S. Constitution

    c. rules issued by the president

    d. laws passed by local governments

2. What does the highest law protect?

    a. the rights of the courts

    b. the rights of Congress

    c. the rights of the president

    d. the rights of American citizens

3. What can happen when people pass a law that does not agree with the Constitution?

    a. The president may order the people to change the law.

    b. Congress may vote on the law and send it to the president.

    c. A court may rule that the law is unconstitutional.

    d. A court may change the Constitution to agree with the law.

LESSON 17: Checks and Balances

 GOAL: To further explore the balance of power in the United States and the controls that are in place

WORDS TO KNOW

acquitted	minors	proposal
convict	pardon	

Checks on the Judicial Branch

As you know, a decision of the Supreme Court is final. There is no higher court, so its rulings cannot be appealed. The Supreme Court is the highest court of the land.

A Supreme Court decision can, however, be overturned by Congress. There is only one way to do this—by amending the Constitution. For example, in 1895, the Supreme Court ruled against an income tax. With an income tax, wealthy people would pay more in taxes than poor people. The Supreme Court ruled that such a tax was not legal. But Congress overturned this ruling with the 16th Amendment to the Constitution. That amendment made an income tax legal.

What can the executive and legislative branches do to check the judicial branch?

The president can use these checks:

- appoint Supreme Court justices

- **pardon**, or set free, people convicted in federal court

Congress can use these checks:

- decide how many federal judges there should be

- decide how much the federal judges' salaries will be

Here is an example of how the president can check the power of the Supreme Court: Suppose the president does not agree with the decisions a Supreme Court is making. If a justice retires, the president will get to choose a replacement. The president can choose a new justice whose principles and interests are close to the president's.

■ PRACTICE 61: Checks on the Judicial Branch

Circle the letter of the correct answer to each of the following questions.

1. Can a Supreme Court ruling be appealed?
   a. yes
   b. no

2. How can Congress overturn a Supreme Court ruling?
   a. by appealing the ruling to a higher court
   b. by overriding the president's veto
   c. by amending the Constitution
   d. by removing justices from the Supreme Court

TIP

Remember what you have already learned about the system of checks and balances. Even though the Supreme Court is the highest court, its power can still be checked by the other two branches. The president, for example, can check the Supreme Court by choosing new justices to fill any openings on the court. Congress can also check the Supreme Court's power—not only by amending the Constitution, but also by approving or rejecting a president's choice of justice.

Checks on the Legislative Branch

What can the executive and judicial branches do to check the legislative branch?

The president can use this check:

■ veto, or refuse to sign, acts that Congress has passed

The Supreme Court can use this check:

- say that an act or a law of Congress is not constitutional

Here is an example of how the president can check the power of Congress. Suppose Congress puts together a new clean air bill. A bill is a **proposal,** or suggestion, for law. Most members of Congress like this bill, and they vote to make it a law. This means that they have passed the clean air bill. The clean air bill then becomes an act. An act is a proposal for law that has been passed by Congress. For the act to become law, it must be signed by the president. The president may think the act is too strict or not strict enough. The president can then veto, or refuse to sign, the act.

IN REAL LIFE

One recent example of the Supreme Court checking the legislative branch happened with the Communications Decency Act (CDA). The CDA was made a law in 1996. The CDA made it illegal to put "indecent" or "offensive" material on the Internet where it could be used by **minors** (people under 18 years of age). Right after the CDA was passed, a group of free speech and computer industry groups filed a lawsuit. They argued that the CDA went against their right to free speech. In 1997, the case went to the Supreme Court. The court decided that the CDA was unconstitutional since it went against the First Amendment to the Constitution, which protects freedom of speech. Congress tried to pass a similar law, the Child Online Protection Act (COPA), in 1998. As of 2004, that law is still being challenged in lower courts.

■ PRACTICE 62: Checks on the Legislative Branch

On the lines provided, write the correct answer to each question.

1. How can the Supreme Court check the legislative branch?

   _____

   _____

2. How can the president check the legislative branch?

_____

_____

Checks on the Executive Branch

What can the legislative and judicial branches do to check the executive branch?

The House of Representatives and the Senate can use these checks:

- refuse to approve money for the president's budget

- refuse to approve the president's choice for many government jobs

- override, or set aside, the president's veto

- impeach the president (accuse him or her of a federal crime)

The Supreme Court can use this check:

- declare the president's actions unconstitutional

Here is an example of how Congress can check the president's power. Let's go back to the clean air act mentioned on page 112. Congress has passed the act, and the president has then vetoed it. But many members of Congress disagree with the president's veto. Congress can vote to override the president's veto. To do this, at least two thirds of both the Senate and the House of Representatives must support the override. If that happens, the clean air act will become law, even though the president has vetoed it.

■ PRACTICE 63: Checks on the Executive Branch

On the lines provided, write the correct answer to each question.

1. What can Congress do if they do NOT agree with a president's veto?

_____

_____

2. How can the Supreme Court check the executive branch?

_____

_____

_____

To *impeach* means to accuse a federal official of treason (helping the country's enemies), bribery, or another high crime. The House of Representatives can vote to impeach a president. If that happens, the president is then put on "trial" before the Senate. This trial is just like one in court, except that the jury is very large—all 100 members of the Senate. If at least two thirds of the Senate (67 senators) vote to **convict** (find him or her guilty), the president is removed from office.

You may have heard about the case of President Richard M. Nixon and the Watergate scandal of 1973–74. Nixon was not actually impeached, but he was the first president ever to resign.

Only two presidents have been impeached. President Andrew Johnson was impeached in 1868 for firing the secretary of war without approval from the Senate. Johnson was put on trial by the Senate. He was found not guilty, but he was **acquitted** (found not guilty) by only one vote! Johnson remained in office, but his party asked him not to run for a second term as president.

President Bill Clinton was also voted by the House to be impeached. He was accused of giving false testimony and obstruction of justice. After being put on trial in 1998, Clinton was acquitted by the Senate. The vote on the first charge was 55 to 45 to aquit, and 50 to 50 (an aquittal) on the second charge.

Balance of Power

Look at the flowchart below. This chart uses arrows to show relationships among the three branches of government. Each solid line connects a branch of government to its activities. Each broken arrow connects an activity to the branch that this activity checks.

For example, note the solid line that connects *Supreme Court* to *can declare acts or laws unconstitutional.* This is one of the Supreme Court's activities. A broken arrow then connects this activity to *Congress.* This means that the Supreme Court can check Congress by declaring its acts or laws unconstitutional.

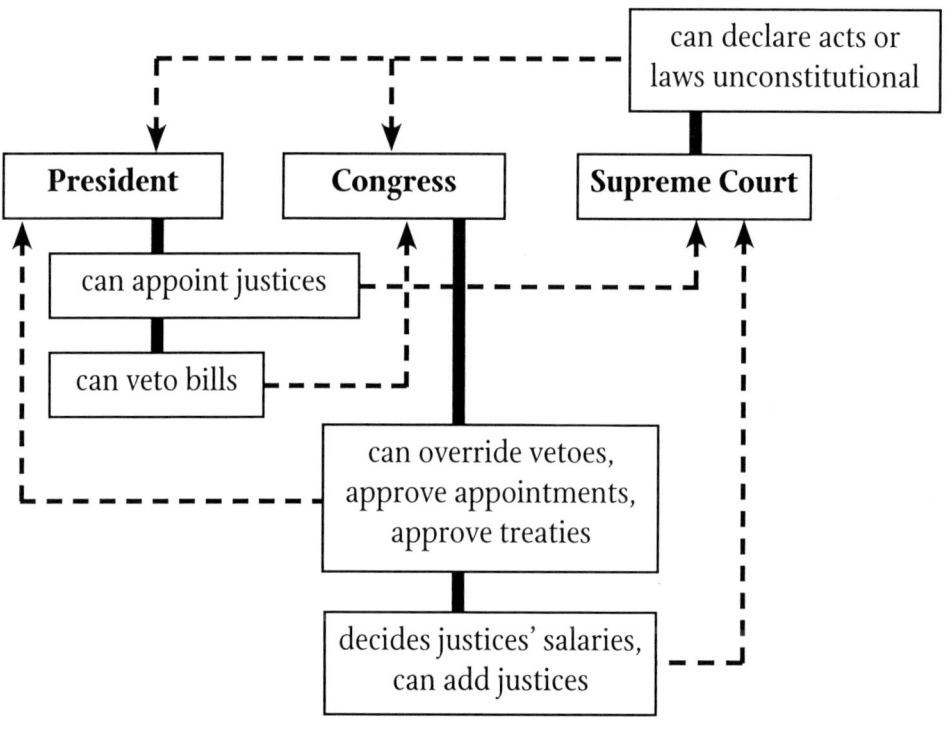

■ PRACTICE 64: Balance of Power

Use the flowchart on page 115 to help you match each activity in column A to a check in column B. Write the correct letter on the line.

Column A

_____ 1. President can veto a law

_____ 2. Congress can override a president's veto.

_____ 3. President chooses justices

_____ 4. Supreme Court can declare laws unconstitutional

_____ 5. Congress can change the number of justices.

Column B

a. executive check on judicial branch

b. executive check on legislative branch

c. judicial check on legislative branch

d. legislative check on executive branch

e. legislative check on judicial branch

Keeping Democracy Strong

Now you understand checks and balances. You also understand separation of powers. These two plans keep any one person, or group of people, from getting too much power in the U.S. government. This was the intention of the framers of the Constitution. They wanted to create a strong government for the United States. They also wanted to limit the power of the government.

What would happen if there were no separation of powers? One person or a small group would have all the power. This person or group could make laws, enforce them, and interpret them; they could pass any law they wanted. They could choose to enforce some laws and not others. And when a citizen was accused of breaking a law, this person or group could also judge the citizen in court. This type of government would be more like a dictatorship than a democracy.

What would happen if there were no checks and balances? Each branch of government could do whatever it pleased. For example, Congress could pass any law it wanted. There would be no one to stop Congress from passing laws that went against the rights and freedoms of citizens.

Separation of powers helps to prevent one person or group from taking over our country. So do checks and balances. They keep our democracy strong.

■ PRACTICE 65: Keeping Democracy Strong

Circle the letter of the correct answer to each of the following questions.

1. Why is separation of powers important to our democracy?
   a. It makes sure that one group has all of the power.
   b. It helps to keep any one group from taking too much power.
   c. It makes sure that no one has any power.

2. What could happen without checks and balances in government?
   a. Each branch of government could do whatever it wanted.
   b. Each branch of government would help check the other branches' power.
   c. Every branch of government would have an equal amount of power.

IN REAL LIFE

You have probably seen parts of major court cases on the television news. What you may not know is that you, as an American citizen, have the right to observe many court sessions in your own local courts. Watching a trial in person can help you understand the judicial process from a whole new perspective. To find out about court sessions in your area, call the administrative office of your local courts. These numbers should be listed in the state government section of your phone book.

UNIT 4 REVIEW

Circle the letter of the correct answer to each of the following questions.

1. Which branch of government is Congress?
    a. executive
    b. legislative
    c. judicial
    d. bicameral

2. Which of the following is NOT a duty of the president?
    a. enforcing laws
    b. appointing heads of executive departments
    c. breaking ties in the Senate
    d. approving or vetoing bills passed by Congress

3. Which of the following correctly describes the National Science Foundation, the U.S. Commission on Civil Rights, and the EPA?
    a. state organizations
    b. executive departments
    c. independent agencies
    d. part of the president's Cabinet

4. What happens to a bill right after it is introduced to Congress?
    a. Both houses of Congress vote on it.
    b. It is sent to the president.
    c. It is amended.
    d. It is sent to a committee to be studied.

5. Which is the lowest court in the federal court system?
    a. district court
    b. state court
    c. circuit court
    d. Supreme Court

6. Which set of actions turns a bill into a law?
    a. It is passed by both houses of Congress and signed by the president.
    b. It is passed by at least one house of Congress and signed by the president.
    c. It is passed by both houses of Congress.
    d. It is passed by at least one house of Congress.

7. What is a precedent?
    a. an opinion of the Supreme Court
    b. a case involving a crime
    c. decisions by judges in past cases
    d. a case involving a dispute

8. How is a civil case different from a criminal case?
    a. Civil cases do not involve a crime.
    b. Civil cases do not involve a dispute.
    c. Civil cases do not involve a court.
    d. Civil cases do not involve precedents.

9. What does it mean to "enact a law"?
    a. to enforce a law
    b. to interpret a law
    c. to pass a law
    d. to veto a law

10. What is the supreme law of the United States?
    a. the Cabinet
    b. the president
    c. Congress
    d. the Constitution

UNIT 4 APPLICATION ACTIVITY
Your Senators and Representative

You are represented in Congress by two senators from your state, and by one representative from the congressional district in which you live. Find out the names and addresses of these three people, and record that information below.

Senator (name): _____

Address: _____

_____

Senator (name): _____

Address: _____

_____

Representative (name): _____

Address: _____

_____

Next, prepare to write a letter to one of your senators or your representative. First, think about a current issue that concerns you. What are your main concerns? What main points do you want to make in your letter? Do you have any suggestions or solutions to offer? Write some of your ideas on the lines below. Then, write the letter and send it.

_____

_____

_____

_____

_____

UNIT 5
The Presidential Election Process

LESSON 18: Presidential Elections

WORDS TO KNOW

ballot	inauguration	popular vote
election	national convention	
electoral vote	party delegates	

The Primary Elections

The office of president is our nation's highest. Every four years, there is an election for president. An **election** is the process of voting for someone to hold a position. In an election, different candidates run against each other to win the position. The one who receives the most votes wins.

The process for electing a U.S. president starts with primary elections. The purpose of primary elections is for each political party to choose a presidential candidate. You can think of the primary elections as the "first round" of a presidential election. The winners of each party's primary elections will then run against each other in the general election.

Most states hold their own primary election. Voters select the presidential hopeful they want to represent their party in the general election. Presidential hopefuls campaign for the chance to be their party's candidate. They campaign from state to state.

Some states hold a caucus instead of a primary. In a caucus, all the members of a political party hold a meeting in each town in the state. At the meeting, people vote for their candidate by a show of hands or by standing as a group. A caucus has the same result as a primary, but it is much less formal. Other business besides voting for candidates may take place at a caucus, as well.

You have already learned that in a representative democracy, citizens vote for representatives who make decisions for them. The same thing happens when electing a president and vice president. The American people do not vote directly for the president and vice president in the primary election. Instead, they vote for representatives. These representatives then cast the formal vote. The representatives in primary elections are called **party delegates.** When you vote for a candidate in a primary election, you are really voting for delegates.

After the primary elections, delegates from each state go to their party's **national convention.** Each political party holds its own national convention. In 2004, for example, the Republican Party held their national convention in New York City. Republican delegates from each state came to this convention. At the convention, the delegates vote for a candidate. The person who receives the most votes becomes that party's candidate for president. In 2004, delegates at the Republican National Convention elected George W. Bush as their candidate for president.

IN REAL LIFE

There are two main political parties in the United States. But there are also many smaller parties that you may not know about. In the 2000 presidential election, there were 11 parties with presidential candidates. Here is a list of all the parties.

- American Party
- Constitution Party
- Green Party
- Independent Party
- Libertarian Party
- Natural Law Party

- Prohibition Party
- Reform Party
- Socialist Party USA
- Socialist Workers Party
- Workers World Party

■ PRACTICE 66: The Primary Elections

Circle the letter of the correct answer to each of the following questions.

1. How often is a U.S. president elected?
   a. every year
   b. every four years
   c. every eight years
   d. whenever Congress calls for an election

2. What is the purpose of primary elections?
   a. to elect a president and vice president
   b. to elect senators and representatives for Congress
   c. to choose candidates for the general election
   d. to determine the date of the general election

3. The following people are all U.S. citizens. Which person might NOT be able to vote in her state's primary election?
   a. Hannah is registered with the Republican Party.
   b. Keisha is registered with the Democratic Party.
   c. Mishtu is registered with the Libertarian Party.
   d. Lisa has not registered with any political party.

4. What is the role of party delegates at the national conventions?
   a. to vote in the general election
   b. to choose their party's candidate for president
   c. to campaign from state to state
   d. to plan the primary elections

The General Election

The second part of a presidential election is the general election. The general election is a national election. In this election, candidates from different political parties run against each other. There can also be other candidates who do not represent any particular political party. The general election determines who becomes the president and vice president of the United States.

The general election always takes place in November. It is held on the first Tuesday after the first Monday of the month. This is when U.S. citizens go to their local voting place and vote for the candidate of their choice. These votes are counted in each state. This is called the **popular vote.**

Just as in the primary elections, however, the popular vote is not the final vote. Instead, there is another layer of people who cast the final vote. These people are called electors. Electors are representatives of a political party. When you vote for a presidential candidate, you are actually voting for electors from that candidate's party. This may seem strange, since the **ballot,** or voting sheet, only lists the names of the candidates. Most voters believe they are making the final decision for a presidential candidate.

When a candidate wins a state's popular vote, the electors from that candidate's party win the state's seats in the Electoral College. The Electoral College is made up of all the winning electors in the country. It is the Electoral College that then votes for the president and vice president. This is called the **electoral vote.**

Here is an example: In the 1996 presidential election, residents of Georgia gave Bob Dole (the Republican Party candidate) 1,078,972 votes. They gave President Bill Clinton (the Democratic Party candidate) 1,047,214 votes. They gave Ross Perot (the Reform Party candidate) 146,031 votes. Bob Dole won the popular vote in Georgia. Since Dole was the Republican Party candidate, the Republican electors won Georgia's seats in the Electoral College.

According to tradition, each member of the Electoral College then votes for his or her own party's candidate. In the example above, Georgia's electors would vote for Dole. When this happens, a state's electoral vote reflects its popular vote. However, this is not required by law. Electors can legally vote for any candidate.

Each state gets a certain number of seats in the Electoral College. According to the Constitution, states get as many seats as they have senators and representatives in Congress. Every state has two senators. But the number of representatives a state has depends on its population. States with larger populations have more representatives in Congress. This means that larger states get more seats in the Electoral College.

In 1996, for example, the state of Georgia had 2 senators and 11 representatives in Congress. So, Georgia had 13 seats in the Electoral College. The state of California has a much larger population than Georgia. In 1996, California had 2 senators and 52 representatives in Congress. So, California had 54 seats in the Electoral College. Each member of the Electoral College gets one vote. This means that Georgia had 13 electoral votes and California had 54 electoral votes in 1996.

As of 2012, there are 538 members of the Electoral College. This number comes from adding 100 (senators) plus 435 (representatives) plus 3 (electors from Washington, D.C.). A candidate who receives a majority (at least 270 electoral votes) becomes president of the United States. If no candidate receives a majority, the House of Representatives chooses a president from the top three candidates.

It is possible for a candidate to win the popular vote but not receive enough electoral votes to become president. In the 2000 election, for example, Al Gore won 48.38 percent of the popular vote. George W. Bush won 47.87 percent. But Bush won the popular vote in some states with many Electoral College votes. He received 271 Electoral College votes, compared with 266 for Gore.

The election process finally ends on January 20. This is when the winning candidates take their oaths of office to become president and vice president of the United States. This ceremony is called the presidential **inauguration.**

■ PRACTICE 67: The General Election

Circle the letter of the correct answer to each of the following questions.

1. What happens in a general presidential election?
   a. Candidates from different parties run against each other.
   b. Candidates from the same party run against each other.
   c. Political parties choose their candidate for president.
   d. Each state chooses party delegates.

2. What is the popular vote?
    a. the vote of party delegates
    b. the vote of members of the Electoral College
    c. the vote of the American people
    d. the vote taken at national conventions

3. What is the electoral vote?
    a. the vote of party delegates
    b. the vote of members of the Electoral College
    c. the vote of the American people
    d. the vote taken at national conventions

4. Suppose a state has 2 senators and 20 representatives in Congress. How many electoral votes would this state have?
    a. 18
    b. 20
    c. 22
    d. 24

5. Suppose the Democratic candidate wins the popular vote in Oregon. Oregon has 7 electoral votes. How many of Oregon's electoral votes will be cast by Democrats?
    a. none
    b. 1
    c. 3
    d. all

6. The Electoral College system is an example of what kind of government?
    a. monarchy
    b. dictatorship
    c. direct democracy
    d. representative democracy

Review of Presidential Elections

The presidential election process is very complicated. Here is a flowchart to help you remember each of the main steps.

PRIMARY ELECTIONS

Presidential hopefuls run to represent their parties (state by state).

↓

NATIONAL CONVENTIONS

Parties choose presidential and vice-presidential candidates.

↓

GENERAL ELECTION

Candidates run for offices of president and vice president (nationally).

↓

ELECTORAL VOTE

Members of the Electoral College vote for president and vice president.

↓

INAUGURATION

Winners of the electoral vote become president and vice president of the United States.

■ PRACTICE 68: Review of Presidential Elections

Circle the letter of the correct answer to each of the following questions.

1. Which of the following happens first?
   a. the primary elections
   b. the national conventions
   c. the general election
   d. the inauguration

2. Which of the following is a national election?
   a. primary elections
   b. general election

3. When do the winning candidates actually become president and vice president?
   a. at the national conventions
   b. immediately after the general election
   c. at the inauguration
   d. in November

TIP

To remember the different levels of a presidential election, just compare it to a national sports tournament, such as the World Series. In baseball, the playoffs are like the primary elections. Teams in the American League play each other to see who will get to go to the World Series. Teams in the National League do the same. Each league ends up with its own championship team—like a political party electing its presidential candidate. The championship teams in each league play each other in the World Series. This is like presidential candidates running against each other in the general election. The winner is named the best team in baseball—or the president of the United States!

LESSON 19: The Electoral College

 GOAL: To learn the reasons why the Electoral College exists and how it functions

History of the Electoral College

The founders of our country debated how a president should be elected. Should the voters elect the president directly? Or, should representatives vote on candidates?

The founders worried that most citizens would not know about candidates from different states. In the late 1700s, there were no radios or televisions. There were no cars, airplanes, or trains. Candidates could not debate on television. They could not advertise on radio. They could not travel quickly around the country talking about their ideas.

The founders did not believe that voters in New Hampshire, for example, would know about candidates in Virginia. Voters from Georgia would not know about candidates from New York. For this reason, they set up a system of electors. They believed that electors would learn about all candidates. Therefore, electors would make wiser decisions.

Today, the Electoral College remains. But electors do not really act on their own. Electors usually promise to support a certain candidate in the general election. Then, following tradition, they vote in the Electoral College in the same way as the majority from their state. Only in two states—Maine and Nebraska—do the electors split their votes according to the popular vote in their state.

■ PRACTICE 69: History of the Electoral College

Circle the letter of the correct answer to each of the following questions.

1. What are electors?
   a. representatives
   b. candidates
   c. members of Congress
   d. founders

2. What is the main reason why the founders of the Constitution set up the Electoral College?
   a. They did not trust the American people.
   b. They wanted to be sure that the people voting for president knew about all the candidates.
   c. The U.S. population was very large, and it was too difficult to count all of the votes.
   d. They wanted to take power away from the American people.

Review of the Electoral College System

Here is a flowchart that will help you remember how the Electoral College system works.

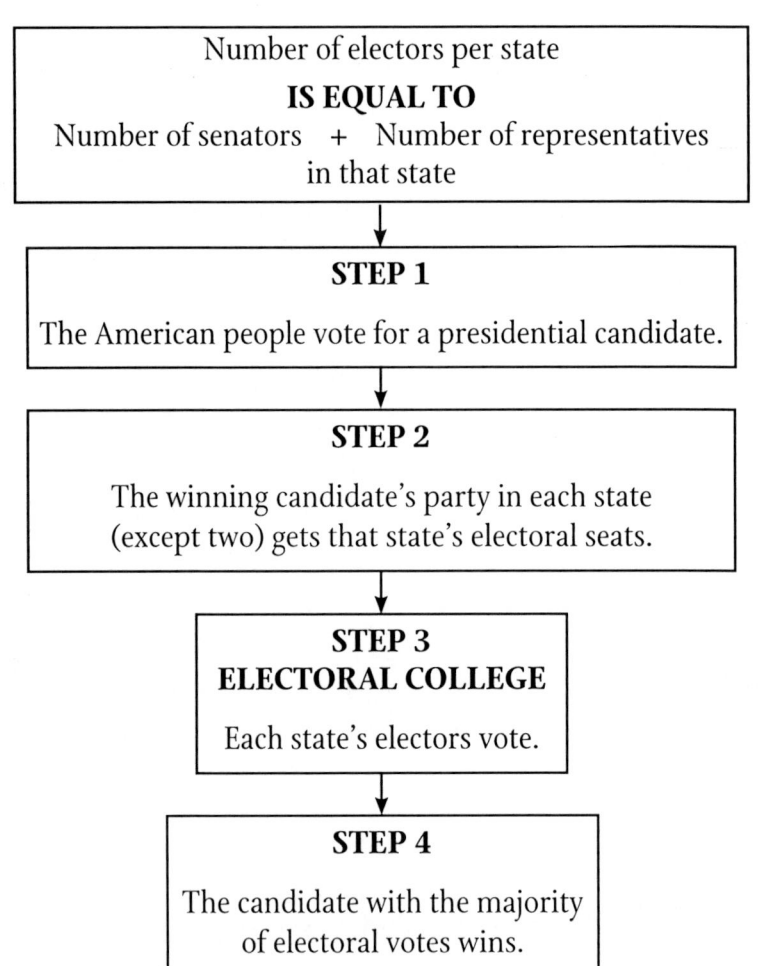

Number of electors per state

IS EQUAL TO

Number of senators + Number of representatives in that state

STEP 1

The American people vote for a presidential candidate.

STEP 2

The winning candidate's party in each state (except two) gets that state's electoral seats.

STEP 3
ELECTORAL COLLEGE

Each state's electors vote.

STEP 4

The candidate with the majority of electoral votes wins.

TIP

If you want to learn more about the Electoral College members in your state, you can call your state's bureau of elections. The bureau's telephone number should be in the state government section of your telephone book. If you cannot find this telephone number, call the local offices of your state representatives or senators. Their telephone numbers will be listed in the "United States Government" section of your phone book, under "Congress, US."

■ PRACTICE 70: Review of the Electoral College System

Use information from the flowchart on page 132 to help you answer the following questions. Circle the letter of the correct answer to each of the following questions.

1. What is the first step in the Electoral College system?
   a. People vote for a presidential candidate.
   b. All of a state's electoral seats go to the party of the winning candidate.
   c. The Electoral College votes.
   d. The candidate with the most electoral votes wins.

2. Which is the last step in the Electoral College system?
   a. People vote for a presidential candidate.
   b. All of a state's electoral seats go to the party of the winning candidate.
   c. The Electoral College votes.
   d. The candidate with the most electoral votes wins.

3. What is the next step after the people vote for the candidates of their choice?
   a. People vote for a vice-presidential candidate.
   b. Each state's electoral seats go to the party of the winning candidate.
   c. The Electoral College votes.
   d. The candidate with the most electoral votes wins.

The Elections of 1824, 1876, 1888, 2000, and 2016

One result of the Electoral College system is that the candidate who wins the popular vote may not always win the election. This has only happened five times in U.S. history—in 1824, 1876, 1888, 2000, and 2016.

In 1824, Andrew Jackson won the popular vote. But Jackson did not receive enough electoral votes to win. At that time, the Electoral College had 261 electors. A candidate needed 131 votes to win. When the votes were counted, these were the results:

Andrew Jackson	99
John Quincy Adams	84
William H. Crawford	41
Henry Clay	37

Since no candidate had 131 votes, the House of Representatives had to decide the election. The House of Representatives chose John Quincy Adams to become president. Andrew Jackson's supporters claimed that Adams had "stolen" the election. Jackson had received more popular votes than Adams. However, Jackson had still lost the election.

In 1876, Samuel Tilden won the popular vote. But he did not have enough electoral votes to become president—he was one vote short. There was a dispute over some of the electoral votes. Tilden lost the dispute, so Rutherford B. Hayes became president.

In 1888, Grover Cleveland won the popular vote with 5,540,050 votes. Benjamin Harrison received only 5,444,337 votes. But Harrison won 233 electoral votes, while Cleveland got only 168. Harrison became president.

In 2000, Al Gore won the popular vote with 50,996,897 votes. George W. Bush received 50,456,002 votes. Yet, Bush won 271 electoral votes, while Gore got only 266. Bush became president.

In 2016, Hillary Clinton won the popular vote with 65,853,514 votes. Donald Trump received 62,984,828 votes. But Trump won 304 electoral votes, while Clinton got only 227. Trump became president.

The state that made the biggest difference in the 2000 election was Florida, which has 25 electoral votes. Bush won the Florida election by only 537 votes. Some voters thought that the ballots had been counted badly. The Democratic candidate, Al Gore, requested that the votes from certain parts of Florida be counted by hand. However, the U.S. Supreme Court decided that a recount of only part of the ballots would be unfair. The Court refused to let the recount happen. Gore went on national television to say he agreed that George W. Bush had won the election.

■ PRACTICE 71: The Elections of 1824, 1876, 1888, 2000, and 2016

Circle the letter of the correct answer to each of the following questions.

1. When no candidate receives a majority of the electoral votes, who decides the election?
   a. the Senate
   b. the Supreme Court
   c. the American people
   d. the House of Representatives

2. What do the elections of 1824, 1876, 1888, 2000, and 2016 show about candidates who win the popular vote?
   a. They are always elected by the House of Representatives.
   b. They do not always win the election.
   c. They always win the majority of electoral votes.
   d. They always win the election.

Objections to the Electoral College

Some people believe that the Electoral College is not a good way to elect a president. They believe that the true choice of the American people is not always reflected in the electoral vote.

Here are three major objections to the Electoral College system:

- A candidate who wins the popular vote can still lose the election. This has happened in the past, and it could happen again.

- No federal law says that an elector must vote with his or her state's majority. In other words, electors can vote any way they want. This rarely happens, but it is possible.

- Electors have the final voting power, not the American people. This means that the election for president is not direct democracy. Representatives, not voters, elect the president.

■ PRACTICE 72: Objections to the Electoral College

Check each item below that states one of the three main objections to the Electoral College system.

☐ **1.** A candidate who wins the popular vote can still lose the election.

☐ **2.** The election of president and vice president is not accomplished by direct democracy.

☐ **3.** Electors never vote the same way as their state's majority.

☐ **4.** Names of electors are secret, so electors can fool the public.

☐ **5.** No national law requires electors to vote with their state's majority.

Population and the Electoral College

Over 50 percent of the U.S. population lives in nine states. They are (from highest to lowest) California, Texas, New York, Florida, Illinois, Pennsylvania, Ohio, Michigan, and New Jersey. These are the states with the largest populations.

Less than 2.5 percent of our country's population lives in another group of ten states. They are (from lowest to highest) Wyoming, Vermont,

Alaska, North Dakota, South Dakota, Delaware, Montana, Rhode Island, Hawaii, and New Hampshire. These are the states with the smallest populations.

What does population mean in terms of the Electoral College?

First of all, it means that the nine largest states hold a big part of the electoral votes. These votes give the large states a lot of influence. On the other hand, every state gets at least three electors. So, even small states have more influence with the Electoral College system than they would without it. In 2004, Vermont had a population of only 608,890 people, or 0.22 percent of the U.S. population. But Vermont's three electors gave it 0.6 percent of the electoral vote. So, because of the Electoral College system, Vermont has a greater voice in national elections than it would otherwise.

THINK ABOUT IT

Would a candidate be more likely to ignore a large state or a small state? Explain. Write your answer on a separate sheet of paper.

■ PRACTICE 73: Population and the Electoral College

Write the answers to each question on the lines provided.

1. Name two of the nine states that have the fewest electors in the Electoral College.

   _____

2. Name two of the nine states that have the most electors in the Electoral College.

   _____

3. How does population affect the Electoral College?

   _____

   _____

Arguments for the Electoral College

Some people believe that the Electoral College is a good system for electing a president and vice president. Here are three main reasons for supporting the Electoral College system:

- The Electoral College gives small states a bigger voice. Every state gets at least three electors. So, candidates are more likely to think about the small states. A small state could make a difference in a close election.

- The Electoral College balances the needs of large and small states. Large states have more influence. However, smaller states have a voice, too.

- The Electoral College system helps prevent a disputed election. The popular vote may be very close. In a close election, the losing candidate may ask for a recount. Recounting the vote can take many weeks.

In a presidential election, a recount could lead to even greater problems. The winner might not be named by January 20. Who would be president? With the Electoral College system, the results are usually clear. Even in a close election, there is a winner. In 1960, John F. Kennedy got only 118,574 more popular votes than Richard M. Nixon. This is a very small number when compared to the whole U.S. voting population. But it was clear that Kennedy won the Electoral College vote, with 303 votes to Nixon's 219.

An unusual situation happened in the 2000 presidential election. Republicans and Democrats disputed the results in Florida. Many ballots were challenged, and counting and recounting of the vote continued for more than a month. The outcome of the presidential election remained uncertain during this time, because whichever candidate won Florida's Electoral College vote would win the national electoral vote. On December 12, the U.S. Supreme Court ordered an end to the recounts, with Republican George W. Bush leading in the popular vote at that time. Bush won Florida by 537 votes in the final, still disputed official Florida count. This gave Bush a total of 271 Electoral College votes, compared with 266 for Democrat Al Gore. Gore, however, won the nationwide popular vote by about 500,000.

■ PRACTICE 74: Arguments for the Electoral College

Check each statement that gives a reason for keeping the Electoral College system.

☐ **1.** A candidate who wins the popular vote can still lose the election.

☐ **2.** The results of the Electoral College vote are clear.

☐ **3.** A disputed election could leave the country without a president.

☐ **4.** Names of electors are secret, so electors can fool the public.

☐ **5.** No federal law requires electors to vote with the state's majority.

You have now learned the main arguments for and against the Electoral College system. What do you think? Should this country still use this system? In the space below, write an essay in support of your position for or against the Electoral College system.

_____

_____

_____

_____

_____

_____

_____

LESSON 20: Choosing the Best Candidate

GOAL: To understand how to be a well-informed voter

WORDS TO KNOW

media   "sound bites"

How to Choose Your President

Learning about presidential candidates takes some work. But it is your duty as a citizen to be informed.

You can get your facts about the candidates from different places. Many voters rely on television news. Television news gives only a small part of the story, though. Read other **media** sources, too, such as newspapers and magazines. Gather brochures from each candidate's office. Visit the official web sites of the candidates and their political parties. Make sure you understand what each candidate thinks about the issues that concern you.

Keep your mind open. Talk to others about the election. However, be careful to base your decisions on facts. Do not let the opinions of others change your mind unless you take the time to think them through.

■ PRACTICE 75: How to Choose Your President

Check each of the following statements that show an informed voter.

☐ **1.** "I trust my candidate because of the way she speaks."

☐ **2.** "I will vote for him because of the honest look in his eyes."

☐ **3.** "I like my candidate because of her stand on welfare."

☐ **4.** "I will vote for my candidate because he seems nice."

☐ **5.** "I get all of my information from television news."

When you are learning about presidential candidates, try making a chart to organize your facts. Along the top, list the names of the candidates. Along the left side, list the type of information you want to gather about each candidate. Here is an example.

	Candidate A	**Candidate B**	**Candidate C**
Political party			
Voting record			
Experience			
Stand on the Issues			

Voters and the Media

What makes voters choose one candidate over another?

Researchers find that personality matters. Today, voters worry a lot about what kind of person a candidate is. The candidate's party, voting record, experience, and ideas are less important. In 1960, two thirds of all voters voted only for candidates who belonged to their chosen party. Today, the number has dropped to one third.

Some experts say that television has brought about these changes. More and more Americans rely on television news to learn about the candidates in a presidential election. Television cameras let viewers see their candidates up close. So, viewers react with their feelings. In other words, personality counts.

Also, the nature of television has changed how Americans learn about the candidates. For example, television news programs rely on short news stories with interesting pictures to keep viewers interested. To get on television, candidates must create "media events." They must also keep their messages short and interesting. A television station is not going to play a candidate's 10-minute speech on the news. At most, they will play only 5 or 10 seconds of it. So, candidates try to talk in **"sound bites"**—

short, interesting phrases that will play well on the news. This makes it difficult for voters to learn how candidates stand on complex issues.

■ PRACTICE 76: Voters and the Media

Answer each of the following.

1. Check each response that is based more on issues than on personality.

    ☐ **a.** "I will not vote for a candidate without experience in foreign affairs."

    ☐ **b.** "I will not vote for someone who does not look tall and strong."

    ☐ **c.** "I will not vote for someone who is against capital punishment."

    ☐ **d.** "I will not vote for someone who looks too old."

2. Which of the following is FALSE? Circle the letter of the correct answer.

    a. More and more Americans learn about presidential candidates on television.

    b. Many people feel that television has influenced the election process.

    c. Candidates must talk in "sound bites" if they want to get on the television news.

    d. Television news coverage makes it easy to learn how candidates stand on complex issues.

■ IN REAL LIFE

You have already learned that the presidential election of 1960 was very close. This election may have also been the first one influenced greatly by television. In this election, John F. Kennedy ran against Richard M. Nixon. For the first time in U.S. history, the two candidates debated each other on television. During the debate, Kennedy appeared handsome and confident. Nixon, who was older than Kennedy, looked nervous and gruff. Many people feel that Kennedy's appearance during the televised debate helped him win the election.

UNIT 5 REVIEW

Circle the letter of the correct answer to each of the following questions.

1. What is the purpose of primary elections?
   a. to select the president and vice president
   b. to select presidential candidates for the general election
   c. to select electors for the Electoral College
   d. to select members of the House of Representatives

2. What is the popular vote?
   a. the vote of the Electoral College
   b. the vote of party delegates
   c. the vote of the American people
   d. the vote of representatives

3. What is an elector?
   a. any citizen who votes in an election
   b. anyone who works for the federal government
   c. a group of representatives who work in the Senate
   d. a member of the Electoral College

4. How is the number of electors calculated for each state?
   a. It is equal to the number of that state's representatives.
   b. It is equal to the number of that state's senators and representatives.
   c. It is equal to the number of that state's senators.
   d. It is equal to the number of federal employees working for that state.

5. Suppose a state has 44 electors. Which of the following would be TRUE about this state?
   a. The state has 42 senators in Congress.
   b. The state has 44 federal employees.
   c. The state has 44 senators and representatives in Congress.
   d. none of the above

6. Which of the following is an argument in favor of the Electoral College?
    a. It is not an example of direct democracy.
    b. No federal law requires an elector to vote with the state's majority.
    c. The results are always clear.
    d. A candidate can win the popular vote and still lose the election.

7. Which of the following is an argument against the Electoral College?
    a. It does not directly represent the popular vote.
    b. The results are always clear.
    c. The needs of big and small states are balanced.
    d. Small states are not so easily ignored.

8. What do the elections of 1824, 1876, 1888, 2000, and 2016 show?
    a. that electors do not always choose the best candidate
    b. that candidates who win the popular vote do not always win the election
    c. that candidates who win the popular vote always win the election
    d. that electors always vote with the majority of their state

9. What have researchers found to be most important to today's voters?
    a. the voting record of the candidates
    b. the personality of the candidates
    c. the experience of the candidates
    d. the ideas of the candidates

10. Which of the following statements shows a responsible voter?
    a. "I will not vote for any candidate who looks weak or sleazy."
    b. "I will vote for this candidate because I agree with his stands on the issues."
    c. "I get all of my information about the candidates from television news."
    d. "I will vote for that candidate because she looks honest."

UNIT 5 APPLICATION ACTIVITY
The Perfect President

The president of the United States is the highest officer in the country. What qualities do you think would make the perfect president? What kind of experience would he or she have? What changes would he or she support? Also, think about the personality of this person. Would he or she come across as tough and determined? Or, would he or she be gentle and kindhearted? On the lines below, explain the qualities that you think would make the perfect president. Use another sheet of paper, if needed.

What kind of experience would he or she have? _____

_____

_____

_____

_____

What kind of personality would he or she have? _____

_____

_____

_____

_____

Is the president's appearance important? If so, how would the president look? What age would he or she be?

_____

_____

_____

_____

Choose two issues that are important to you. Some examples are unemployment, minority rights, taxes, pollution, or homeless people. How would your perfect president feel about these two issues? What changes would he or she make?

_____

_____

_____

_____

_____

Optional Activity: Now, do some research. Have any of our past presidents come close to your ideal? Who comes closest? Explain your choice below.

_____

_____

_____

_____

_____

_____

_____

_____

_____

_____

_____

_____

_____

_____

_____

UNIT 6

State Government

LESSON 21: Our Fifty States

GOAL: To recognize the diversity of the fifty United States and their need for individual state governments

Our Fifty States

The United States now has fifty states. Look at the map below. You will see that each state is different in size and shape. Rhode Island, at 1,045 square miles, is the smallest. Alaska is the largest state. It spreads across 571,951 square miles.

Geography also differs from state to state. The giant Rocky Mountains run through several states. The mighty Mississippi River cuts through many others. Two great oceans lap the shores of nearly one third of the states, and water surrounds the islands of Hawaii.

The resources of the states vary, too. Some states hold oil, coal, and natural gas. Others have huge forests, rich soil, and grassy plains. Giant farms and ranches fill some states. Others have factories and large cities.

No two states are alike. Each state has a special history. Each state has special needs, too. Therefore, each state has its own constitution. Each state runs its own government. Each state elects its own representatives. In this way, every state government serves its own citizens.

■ PRACTICE 77: Our Fifty States

Answer each of the following questions.

1. What do all fifty states have in common? Circle the letter of the correct answer.
   a. They all have the same resources.
   b. They all have similar geography.
   c. They all have their own government.
   d. They all have the same history.

2. Which state is the largest? _____

3. Which state is the smallest? _____

4. As you know, there are many differences among the fifty states. In what way could these differences be a strength? In what way could they be a weakness? Explain.

   _____

   _____

   _____

   _____

   _____

   _____

   _____

   _____

   _____

   _____

   _____

   _____

LESSON 22: About State Government

 GOAL: To learn the basic structure and function of state government and the role that citizens play

WORDS TO KNOW

initiative	petition	referendum
jury duty	recall	

Branches of State Government

States had governments when they were still English colonies. Each had a charter that set up a government. After the colonies became independent from England, each new state wrote its own constitution, often based on the original charter. These constitutions set up each state's government.

Every state has a government. State government is democratic. This means that citizens vote for their state representatives. In turn, these state representatives make decisions for the citizens. In most states, citizens also vote directly on some issues.

State government is like the federal government in several ways. First, every state government has three branches:

- the executive branch

- the legislative branch

- the judicial branch

State government also has separation of powers. This means that each branch of state government has different powers and responsibilities. Finally, a system of checks and balances keeps any one branch of state government from getting too much power.

■ PRACTICE 78: Branches of State Government

Circle the letter of the correct answers to each of the following questions. (*Hint:* There is more than one correct answer to each question.)

1. Which of the following is a branch of state government?
   a. the executive branch
   b. the legislative branch
   c. the judicial branch
   d. the democratic branch

2. How is state government like the federal government?
   a. They both have three branches.
   b. They both have separation of powers.
   c. They both require citizens to vote directly on all issues.
   d. They both have checks and balances.

State Government "By the People"

Just like the federal government, state government is run "by the people." This means that citizens control their state government. For the system to work, citizens must have certain responsibilities. They must obey state laws. They must pay taxes. Citizens should also do this:

- respect the rights of others

- stay informed about state government

- take part in state government

- vote

Voting is an important way for citizens to have a say in state government. Voting is both a right and a responsibility. State government cannot force a citizen to vote. But if citizens do not vote, the government will not be able to represent their needs and wishes.

Jury duty, however, is a requirement. Every citizen must serve on a jury when called (unless the court agrees to excuse a person from serving). Serving on a jury means going to court, listening to evidence in a case, and helping to make a decision.

■ PRACTICE 79: State Government "By the People"

Circle the letter of the correct answer to each of the following questions.

1. Which of the following is a responsibility of citizens?
   a. respecting the rights of others
   b. voting
   c. obeying state laws
   d. all of the above

2. In what way are voting and jury duty different?
   a. Only voting is a requirement.
   b. Only jury duty is a requirement.
   c. Both voting and jury duty are requirements.
   d. Neither voting nor jury duty is a requirement.

State Constitutions

Each state has its own constitution. Each state constitution is a written document, like the U.S. Constitution. Each one contains the rules for running that state's government.

State constitutions are also like the U.S. Constitution in other ways. For example, most state constitutions have the following four sections:

■ a Preamble, which introduces the constitution

■ a Bill of Rights, which states the freedoms and rights of citizens

■ a state government section, which describes the three branches of government

■ an amendment section, which explains how the state constitution can be changed

No state constitution is above the U.S. Constitution. The U.S. Constitution is the highest law of the land. No state law can go against it.

■ PRACTICE 80: State Constitutions

Circle the letter of the correct answer to each of the following questions.

1. Which information would you probably NOT find in a state constitution?
   a. a description of the state legislative branch
   b. an explanation of the freedom of speech of citizens
   c. a list of businesses in the state
   d. a description of the powers of the state executive branch

2. Which of the following would introduce a state constitution?
   a. the Preamble
   b. the Bill of Rights
   c. the state government section
   d. the amendment section

Direct Democracy

Many states give citizens a chance to practice direct democracy. In other words, citizens have a direct say on some state issues.

States have different ways to give citizens a direct say. Three are described below.

- Initiative—An **initiative** is a proposed solution to a problem in the state. Citizens launch an initiative themselves. To do this, they must first write a petition. A **petition** is a statement that is passed around for people to sign. When a person signs the petition, it means that he or she supports the initiative. If enough people sign the petition, there will be a vote. If at least one half of the voters favor the initiative, it becomes law.

- Referendum—A vote on a special issue is called a **referendum.** For example, a referendum is held when an amendment is proposed to the state constitution. This allows citizens to vote directly on the amendment. Referendums can also be held if the legislature wants citizens to decide a certain issue.

- Recall—A **recall** is a special vote held to remove someone from office. Many citizens must sign a petition before there can be a recall.

■ PRACTICE 81: Direct Democracy

Circle the letter of the word that correctly completes each of the following statements.

1. A vote on a special issue is called a(n) _____.
    a. initiative
    b. referendum
    c. recall
    d. solution

2. When citizens vote on a proposed solution to a problem in their state, they are voting on a(n) _____.
    a. initiative
    b. referendum
    c. recall
    d. solution

3. Before citizens can vote on an initiative, they must write a(n) _____.
    a. referendum
    b. solution
    c. initiative
    d. petition

4. A special vote to remove someone from office is called a(n) _____.
    a. initiative
    b. referendum
    c. recall
    d. solution

LESSON 23: The Powers of the States

GOAL: To gain a deeper understanding of state government and its three branches

WORDS TO KNOW

appellate courts	governor	secretary of state
attorney general	legislature	state supreme court
delegated	lieutenant governor	treasurer
general trial courts	mandatory	

What Can the States Do?

At the start, our country had only 13 states. These states had many powers that now belong to the federal government. For example, states could make their own money. They could tax goods from other states. They could even have their own armies.

The U.S. Constitution, passed in 1789, gave the federal government more power. Any power not **delegated,** or given, to the federal government belonged to the states. States now have the powers listed below.

- They can set up their own plans for the election of national officers.

- They can approve amendments to the U.S. Constitution.

- They can decide on the setup of their state government.

- They can protect citizens with state police and National Guard.

- They can make rules for transportation within the state.

- They can make rules for business within the state.

- They can make rules for education within the state.

■ PRACTICE 82: What Can the States Do?

Answer each of the following.

1. Which of the following is TRUE? Circle the letter of the correct answer.
   a. States have more power now than when the U.S. Constitution was first written.
   b. States have less power now than when the U.S. Constitution was first written.
   c. States have always had the same amount of power.

2. Check each power that belongs to the states today.
   ☐ a. They can run state businesses.
   ☐ b. They can set up state election plans for national officers.
   ☐ c. They can pass laws for all U.S. citizens.
   ☐ d. They can use state police to protect citizens.
   ☐ e. They can appoint justices to the U.S. Supreme Court.

The State Executive Branch

The state executive branch is in charge of carrying out state laws. The head of a state's executive branch is the **governor**. Most governors belong to a major political party. The duties of a governor include the following:

- enforcing state laws

- advising the state legislature on laws needed

- acting as head of the state National Guard

- pardoning people convicted in state courts

If a governor cannot finish his or her term, the state's **lieutenant governor** takes over. The lieutenant governor holds the second highest state office. There are also other top executive officers. They help the governor run important parts of state government.

- The **attorney general** represents the state in court.

- The **secretary of state** keeps official state records.

- The **treasurer** manages state money.

■ PRACTICE 83: The State Executive Branch

Circle the letter of the correct answer to each of the following questions.

1. Suppose there is a big problem at a state college. Which executive officer would call the National Guard troops to help?
   a. the governor
   b. the treasurer
   c. the secretary of state
   d. the attorney general

2. Suppose someone breaks a state law. Which executive officer would try that person in court?
   a. the governor
   b. the treasurer
   c. the secretary of state
   d. the attorney general

The State Legislative Branch

Every state also has a state legislative branch for making laws. This is called the **legislature.** Most state legislatures are similar to Congress. They have two houses. Only Nebraska has just one house.

The two houses of a state legislature are usually called the Senate and the House of Representatives. Some states use other names for their House of Representatives, such as House of Delegates, Assembly, or State House.

State legislatures vary in size. The Maine House of Representatives, for example, has 151 members. The Alaska Senate has 20 members.

The main job of the legislature is to make laws. Just as in Congress, passing a state law takes several steps. State legislatures follow most of the same steps that Congress does.

■ PRACTICE 84: The State Legislative Branch

Circle the letter of the correct answer to each of the following questions.

1. What is the purpose of a state legislature?
   a. to enforce laws
   b. to make laws
   c. to interpret laws
   d. to veto laws

2. How many states have only one house in their state legislature?
   a. none
   b. one
   c. two
   d. all 50

3. How many steps does it take a state legislature to pass a state law?
   a. none
   b. one
   c. two
   d. several

THINK ABOUT IT

On page 156, you learned that state governments can make rules for transportation within their state. One transportation law that has been passed in many states is the **mandatory** (required) seat-belt law. There are different versions of this law. But the main purpose of all of them is to require drivers and front-seat passengers to wear seat belts. If you or someone in your car is caught without a seat belt, the driver of the car can be charged a fine. Many people support seat-belt laws. They feel that these laws protect people who would not normally wear a seat belt. Other people are against this type of law. They feel that wearing a seat belt is a matter of personal choice. Does your state have a mandatory seat-belt law? Do you think the law is fair? Write your answer on a separate sheet of paper.

The State Judicial Branch

The state judicial branch interprets state laws. This means that they make the meaning of existing laws clear. State courts hear two kinds of cases.

- Civil cases are disagreements. They involve matters that deal with money or property.

- Criminal cases involve crimes. A crime occurs when someone breaks the law. Murder, robbery, and arson (setting a fire on purpose) are examples of crimes.

The lowest courts handle routine matters. These include things such as marriages, divorces, adoptions, traffic tickets, and small claims. Juvenile courts generally handle cases that involve people under 18 years old. These courts usually have judges but no juries.

The next highest courts are **general trial courts.** They handle more serious cases. These cases are heard by a judge and jury. These courts have different names in different states, such as district courts, circuit courts, superior courts, or county courts. The **appellate courts,** or courts of appeal, are the next highest courts. They have no juries. Appellate judges decide whether lower-court trials were fair. The highest state court is the **state supreme court.** Decisions of this court can be appealed only to the U.S. Supreme Court.

IN REAL LIFE

Courts in the United States interpret the law by what is called *judicial review.* Imagine that a state passes a law making it illegal to burn the U.S. flag in protest. Some people think the law violates the right of free speech in the Constitution. The courts of the state will not make a judgment about whether the law is constitutional until someone challenges the law in court. This could happen the next time someone burns a flag in protest and is charged with a crime under the new law. The court that tries the case would make a decision about whether the law is constitutional. Then, a higher court could review that decision on appeal and come to a different decision. Lower courts must accept the decisions of the higher courts.

Structure of the State Judicial Branch

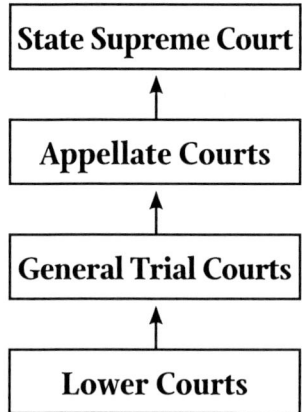

■ PRACTICE 85: The State Judicial Branch

Answer each of the following.

1. Check each case below that would be handled in the lowest state courts.

    ☐ **a.** murder

    ☐ **b.** traffic ticket

    ☐ **c.** robbery

    ☐ **d.** marriage license

2. Suppose that a lawyer does not think that the decision of a general trial court was fair. Where would this lawyer go next? Circle the letter of the correct answer.

    a. the state supreme court

    b. an appellate court

    c. another general trial court

    d. a lower court

LESSON 24: State Income and Expenses

 GOAL: To learn about services provided by the states and how those services are paid for

WORDS TO KNOW

consumer	property tax
consumer protection	public works
corporate tax	sales tax
income tax	service
law enforcement	social welfare programs
maximum security	tolls
minimum security	unemployment pay

Paying for State Services

How do state governments get money to do their work? Some money comes from the federal government. The amount of money a state gets depends on the state's population and needs. Larger states usually get more money from the federal government. Some states also get money by running state businesses. Other states run lotteries.

Taxes are another way for states to get money. A tax is a charge. There are many kinds of taxes. **Sales tax** is a charge put on the goods people buy. **Income tax** is a charge put on the money people earn. **Corporate tax** is a charge put on the money businesses make. **Property tax** is a charge put on the value of land and buildings that people own.

Each state government has many costs. States must pay to run the three branches of government. Also, if you look in the telephone book for your state's offices, you will see that your state provides many services. A **service** is useful work that helps people in the state.

States run hospitals. They build highways and housing. They run welfare programs to help those in need. And as much as one third of a state's money may be used to pay for public education.

Other state costs include health programs and state police. The state also keeps up state parks and forests. State government helps to protect the state's natural resources, too.

■ PRACTICE 86: Paying for State Services

Answer each of the following.

1. Circle the letter of the answer that correctly completes this statement: States get money from all of the following EXCEPT _____.

   a. the federal government

   b. other state governments

   c. taxes

   d. state businesses

2. Which of the following describes a property tax? Circle the letter of the correct answer.

   a. a charge on the goods people buy

   b. a charge on the money people earn

   c. a charge on the value of land and buildings

   d. a charge on the money businesses make

3. Check each service below that state governments must provide.

   ☐ **a.** running the U.S. Supreme Court

   ☐ **b.** repairing state roads

   ☐ **c.** cleaning up state parks

   ☐ **d.** maintaining national landmarks

   ☐ **e.** running state hospitals

   ☐ **f.** amending the U.S. Constitution

   ☐ **g.** paying for public education

   ☐ **h.** protecting national forests

   ☐ **i.** operating the state police force

Many states run lotteries to make money. Some people believe this is wrong. They say that gambling is illegal, and that the states are encouraging people to waste their money. Other people believe that lotteries are an important way for states to make money. They point to all of the programs and services that states pay for with this money. What do you think? Should states run lotteries to make money? Why or why not? Write your answer on a separate sheet of paper.

Education

One of the services that state government provides is education. Most money for public schools comes from city and town governments. But states also give schools money. In fact, state money helps to cover the cost of every student and teacher.

State governments have certain requirements, or demands, for education in their state. State governments decide how long students in their state must go to school. States also decide which subjects all students in their state must study. Requirements are different from state to state.

States are also involved in education in other ways. For example, there are state libraries, colleges, and universities. Some states, like California, have many state colleges. Others have only a few. Some states cover most of the cost for state residents to attend their colleges. Others do not.

IN REAL LIFE

The First Amendment to the U.S. Constitution protects the right of citizens to practice any religion, or none at all. This means that citizens cannot be forced to participate in, agree with, or pay for any religious activities. Since every citizen pays for public schools through their taxes, this means that public schools cannot practice any type of religion. Private schools, however, can practice any type of religion they want. The money for private schools comes from the people who choose to attend them. No one can be forced to attend a private school.

■ PRACTICE 87: Education

Circle the letter of the correct answer to each of the following questions.

1. Where does most of the money for public schools come from?
   a. city and town governments
   b. state governments
   c. the federal government
   d. private donations

2. What type of educational costs do state governments pay for?
   a. money for libraries
   b. money for public schools
   c. money for colleges
   d. all of the above

3. What type of educational system can practice religion?
   a. public schools
   b. private schools
   c. neither private nor public schools

Aid to the Needy

Another service provided by state government is aid to the needy. All states have **social welfare programs.** These programs help citizens in need. Some money for these programs comes from the federal government. But each state must decide how this money is to be spent. The state also must run its own programs. These programs help people to get by. They help people pay for living costs and for finding and paying for housing. Many states also have work programs. These programs offer job training and help people find jobs.

State government also helps out when people lose their jobs. The state gives money to help workers get through hard times. **Unemployment pay** is money given to citizens who have lost their jobs. Unemployment pay only lasts for a certain period of time, or until the person can find a new job. Employers cover most of the cost of unemployment pay.

■ PRACTICE 88: Aid to the Needy

Circle the letter of the correct answer to each of the following questions.

1. Who runs a state's social welfare programs?
   a. the federal government
   b. the state government
   c. the city government
   d. the town government

2. Which people does unemployment pay help?
   a. people who have never worked before
   b. people who are very poor
   c. people who cannot work
   d. people who have lost their jobs

■ THINK ABOUT IT

Social welfare programs are paid for through taxes, so all citizens help pay for them. Some people argue that they should not have to pay for these programs. They say that many people on welfare are able to support themselves. Other people disagree. They say that some people cannot support themselves, such as elderly people, people with disabilities, and single mothers. They also say that many jobs do not offer wages high enough to support a family. What do you think? Should the government provide social welfare programs? Or should everyone have to support themselves? Write your answer on a separate sheet of paper.

Consumer Protection

A third service provided by state government is **consumer protection**. A **consumer** is anyone who buys goods or services. To protect consumers, states keep prices fair on the things that most people need, such as gas, heat, and electricity. Companies that sell these goods and services cannot charge whatever price they want.

States also protect consumers in other ways. They keep advertising honest. Advertisements cannot lie about products or give incorrect prices. States also make sure that food is safe. They do this by setting rules for farms, grocery stores, and restaurants to follow.

■ PRACTICE 89: Consumer Protection

Check each example below that shows how the state helps protect consumers.

☐ **1.** making sure that citizens do not spend their money unwisely

☐ **2.** making sure that every citizen gets to vote

☐ **3.** making sure that advertisements tell the truth about products

☐ **4.** making sure that food sold in stores is handled properly

Public Works

A fourth service provided by state government is **public works.** Every state has buildings, roads, and parks for the public to use. These public areas must be kept clean and safe. Any work done to build, maintain, or repair one of these public areas is considered public works.

Every state has to maintain many state roads, highways, and bridges. States also help their cities set up public transportation systems.

State buildings and lands are also under state control. States construct new government buildings. They make sure that state parks and forests are safe. They protect plants and animals on state lands.

IN REAL LIFE

If you drive, you have probably had to pay **tolls.** A toll is a special charge that a driver must pay to use a highway or bridge. Many states charge tolls on their larger highways and bridges. Tolls help the state pay to keep the roads and bridges clean and safe.

■ PRACTICE 90: Public Works

Check each example of public works below.

- ☐ **1.** repairing state highways
- ☐ **2.** bringing criminals to trial
- ☐ **3.** maintaining campgrounds in state forests
- ☐ **4.** making sure bridges are safe
- ☐ **5.** collecting taxes

State Law Enforcement

A fifth service provided by state government is **law enforcement**. Every state has its own police force. The police force's main job is to patrol state roads. There, state police enforce speed limits. They also help out during emergencies. The governor can send state police anywhere in the state.

State governments also run their own crime labs. These labs help them solve crimes by studying chemicals and materials found at the scene of a crime.

State prisons are also run by the state. There are different kinds of prisons for different crimes.

- **Maximum security** prisons are for prisoners who have committed dangerous crimes, such as murder.

- **Minimum security** prisons are for prisoners who are not considered dangerous to the community.

■ PRACTICE 91: State Law Enforcement

Circle the letter of the correct answer to each of the following questions.

1. What is the main job of a state's police force?
   - **a.** solving crimes
   - **b.** patrolling state roads
   - **c.** protecting the governor
   - **d.** breaking up fights

2. Which type of prison is for people considered dangerous to the community?
   a. maximum security prisons
   b. minimum security prisons

3. Suppose a stained shirt is found at the scene of a crime. Who could study the shirt to help solve the crime?
   a. the minimum security prison
   b. the maximum security prison
   c. the state police force
   d. the state crime lab

State Services Review

State government provides many important services. You have just read about five of them: education, aid to the needy, consumer protection, public works, and law enforcement. Here is a graphic organizer that will help you review these state services and what they provide.

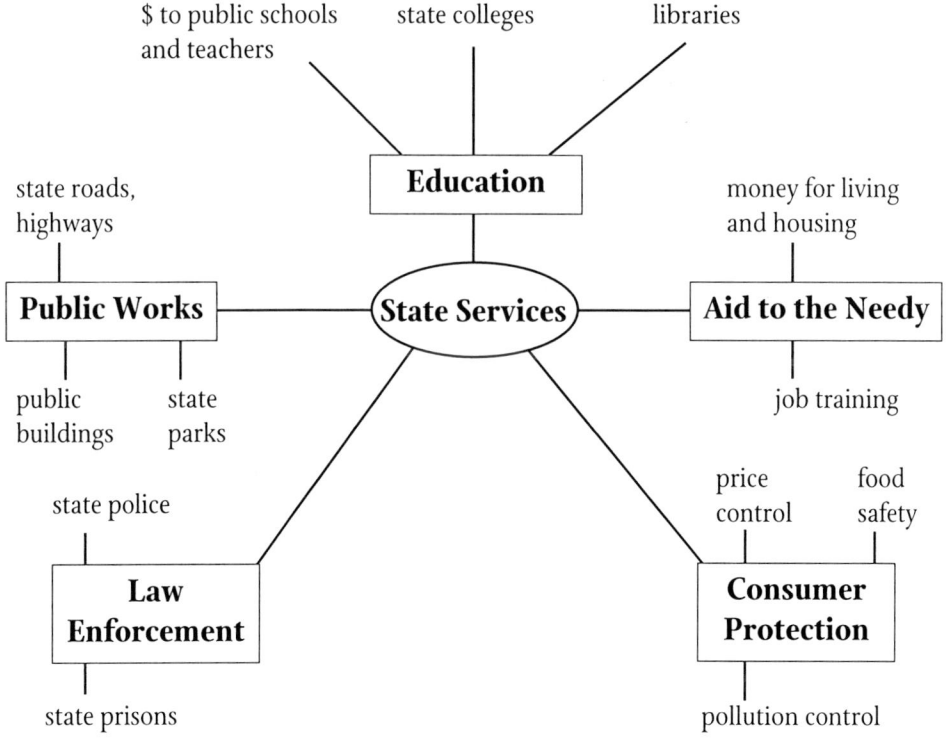

■ PRACTICE 92: State Services Review

Use the graphic organizer on page 169 to answer the questions below. Circle the letter of the correct answer to each question.

1. Which state service makes sure that the food people buy is safe?
   a. aid to the needy
   b. consumer protection
   c. public works
   d. law enforcement
   e. education

2. Which state service makes sure that state roads and bridges are safe?
   a. aid to the needy
   b. consumer protection
   c. public works
   d. law enforcement
   e. education

3. Which state service provides job training?
   a. aid to the needy
   b. consumer protection
   c. public works
   d. law enforcement
   e. education

TIP

As you study the terms in this lesson, it may help to think of similar words that you already know. For example, look at the term *appellate court*. The word *appellate* is related to the word *appeal*. You already know that *appeal* means "request that a verdict be overturned." So, an *appellate court* is where you go when you want the decision of a lower court reconsidered. Looking for familiar words within unfamiliar terms can help you learn and remember the new terms.

UNIT 6 REVIEW

Circle the letter of the correct answer to each of the following questions.

1. Which of the following is a state service?
   a. repairing state roads
   b. making sure the food in restaurants is safe
   c. keeping state beaches clean
   d. all of the above

2. Which of the following is NOT a duty of the governor?
   a. to advise the state legislature on laws needed
   b. to pardon people unfairly convicted of a crime
   c. to interpret laws
   d. all of the above

3. Which of the following is NOT a power that belongs to the states?
   a. approving amendments to the U.S. Constitution
   b. making rules for education throughout the country
   c. setting up state plans for the election of national officers
   d. protecting citizens with state police

4. Who represents the state in court?
   a. the secretary of state
   b. the attorney general
   c. the treasurer
   d. the governor

5. Which of the following is a responsibility of the state?
   a. to protect consumers
   b. to control transportation in the state
   c. to look out for the neediest citizens
   d. all of the above

6. Which statement correctly defines maximum security prisons?
   a. They are for less dangerous criminals.
   b. They are part of the state's consumer protection service.
   c. They are for more dangerous criminals.
   d. They are run by the federal government.

7. Which of the following would introduce a state constitution?
   a. the Preamble
   b. the Bill of Rights
   c. the state government section
   d. the amendments section

8. How many houses do most state legislatures have?
   a. one
   b. two
   c. four
   d. none of the above

9. Which state court hears criminal cases?
   a. state supreme court
   b. lowest court
   c. general trial court
   d. appellate court

10. What is a special vote to remove someone from office?
    a. recall
    b. initiative
    c. referendum
    d. petition

UNIT 6 APPLICATION ACTIVITY
About Your State

How much do you know about your state government? The people who run your state government make decisions that affect your everyday life. They set state taxes, build roads and bridges, set speed limits, and decide which classes you will have to take in school. If you do not know who your state representatives are and what they stand for, you are giving up control of many important decisions.

See how many of the questions that follow you can answer. Then, do some research to answer the ones you do not know. You can use the state government pages of the telephone book to contact offices that will give you information. You can also use your local library, or go to your state's web site on the Internet.

Name of your state: _____

1. Who is your present governor?

   _____

2. How long has this governor been in office?

   _____

3. Who is your present lieutenant governor?

   _____

4. Who is your present attorney general?

   _____

5. Who is your present secretary of state?

   _____

6. Who is your present state treasurer?

   _____

7. How many houses does your state legislature have?

   _____

8. What are the houses called?

   _____

9. How many representatives are in each house?

   _____

10. Who are your state supreme court justices?

    _____

    _____

UNIT 7

Local Government

LESSON 25: What Is Local Government?

GOAL: To learn how local governments are structured and what role citizens can play

WORDS TO KNOW

codes	local government	ordinances
home rule	magistrate courts	protective services
justice courts	municipal courts	special district

Closer to Home

Local government is government that is closest to where you live. The center of the federal government is in Washington, D.C. It is far from many states. The center of each state government is the state capital. Often, it is far from many parts of the state.

Local government is close to the people. Local government keeps "in touch" with citizens. It knows what citizens need. As a result, local government is a link to state government. Local government helps the state understand what its citizens need. Local government helps state government stay "in touch" with the people.

"Local government" can refer to the government of a large area, such as a county, or a smaller area, such as a city, town, or village.

■ PRACTICE 93: Closer to Home

Circle the letter of the correct answer to each of the following questions.

1. Which type of government is closest to where most people live?
   a. federal government
   b. national government
   c. state government
   d. local government

2. How does local government serve as a link to state government?
   a. It helps the state collect taxes.
   b. It helps the state keep in touch with its citizens.
   c. It helps people visit the offices of state government.
   d. It interprets state laws for people.

The Powers of Local Government

Any local government in a state is created by the state government. Each state constitution explains how this may be done. State legislatures decide on county boundaries. They decide the duties of county government. They also decide whether a community can become a city, a town, or a village.

The powers of local government are different from state to state. Some states limit the power of local government. Other states give local government a lot of power. Texas, Nebraska, and Missouri, for example, give communities **home rule.** This means that the state does not interfere in local matters.

Most local governments have the following powers:

- They raise taxes for local purposes.

- They make and enforce local laws.

- They run local services.

TIP

What is the difference between a city, a town, and a village? The main difference is the size of the population. Cities have the largest populations. Towns are in the middle. Villages have the smallest populations. Every state has different population requirements to determine if an area is a city, a town, or a village. So, what is considered a city in North Dakota might be considered only a town in California!

■ PRACTICE 94: The Powers of Local Government

Circle the letter of the correct answer to each of the following questions.

1. Who decides whether a community can become a town?
   a. Congress
   b. the U.S. Supreme Court
   c. the state legislature
   d. the state supreme court

2. What is the term for the power of local government to decide all local matters?
   a. home rule
   b. parish rule
   c. division rule
   d. state legislature

Local Government and Protective Services

Local government provides many **protective services.** These are services that keep people safe and healthy. The list below describes some important protective services provided by local government.

- **Police department:** Police enforce the laws. They patrol streets and highways. They stop crimes, answer emergencies, and work to solve crimes.

- **Fire department:** Firefighters work to put out fires. Fire departments also organize programs to teach young people about fire safety.

- **Water treatment:** Water treatment workers test water to make sure it is clean.

- **Garbage collection:** Garbage collectors remove trash from neighborhoods and businesses.

(continued on next page)

> ■ **Sewage treatment:** Sewage treatment workers clean and get rid of waste matter that is carried in sewers. They make sure that germs from waste matter do not make people sick.
>
> ■ **Local hospitals:** Hospital workers offer medical care to people in their area. They also provide emergency services.

■ PRACTICE 95: Local Government and Protective Services

Check each example of a protective service.

☐ **1.** passing a tax to pay for sewage cleanup

☐ **2.** removing trash from streets on Tuesdays

☐ **3.** finding out who robbed a store

☐ **4.** trying a murder case in court

☐ **5.** giving care to someone hurt in a car accident

Other Services of Local Government

Local government also provides many other important services, such as building local roads and running bus services. The list below describes many services used by citizens every day.

Service	Jobs Done
Public works	builds and maintains local roads and bridges
Traffic control	installs lights, stop signs, and parking meters; sets speed limits; sets up parking lots
Public transportation	runs bus, train, and subway services
Recreation	builds and maintains parks, playgrounds, museums, pools, and libraries

■ PRACTICE 96: Other Services of Local Government

Circle the letter of the correct answer to each of the following questions.

1. Which of the following services do local government departments provide?
   a. building roads and bridges
   b. putting in parking lots
   c. running the city bus system
   d. all of the above

2. Which of the following is NOT an example of public transportation?
   a. subways
   b. trains
   c. taxis
   d. buses

Local Laws

Making laws is an important duty of local government. Local laws are called **ordinances,** or **codes.** There are many kinds of local laws. Some of them are listed below.

- ■ **Theft laws** set penalties for people who steal.

- ■ **Vandalism laws** set penalties for people who destroy the property of others.

- ■ **Traffic laws** help to prevent accidents.

- ■ **Health codes** protect people from sickness.

- ■ **Arson laws** set penalties for people who set fires on purpose.

The city council or county board makes most local laws. First, a council or board member proposes an idea for a law. Then, the council or board researches the proposal and considers many questions. Is the law needed? Will the law solve a current problem? Can the law be enforced, or carried out? What will it cost to enforce the law? Will the law interfere with people's rights? Citizens also get a chance to have input on the proposed law. Sometimes, the board will change the proposal in response to citizens' input. Finally, the council or board votes on the proposed law. If enough members want the law, it passes.

■ PRACTICE 97: Local Laws

Circle the letter of the correct answer to each of the following questions.

1. Which of the following is NOT true?
    a. Local laws are often called ordinances.
    b. Local laws are designed to help keep people safe.
    c. Local laws help to keep property safe.
    d. Local laws must be signed by the governor.

2. Which question would a council member ask about a proposed law?
    a. Is the law necessary?
    b. How much money will it cost to enforce the law?
    c. Will the law interfere with people's rights?
    d. all of the above

Local Courts

Local courts settle disputes. They punish criminals and award money to people who have been hurt.

Small communities have only two kinds of local courts: magistrate and justice. **Magistrate courts** try minor cases. These are cases that involve small sums of money (usually less than $100). **Justice courts** try more serious cases, such as burglaries. The most serious cases are tried by the state's general trial courts.

Large communities have a system of **municipal courts,** or city courts. Just as in the smaller communities, the most serious cases are tried by the state's general trial courts. For the less serious cases, there are six types of municipal courts, listed below.

■ **Civil courts** handle disputes between citizens.

■ **Criminal courts** handle cases involving a crime.

■ **Traffic courts** handle broken traffic or parking rules.

- **Small-claims courts** handle cases that involve small sums of money (mostly less than $500).

- **Juvenile courts** handle cases involving people under 18 years of age.

- **Divorce courts** handle matters concerning the breakup of marriages.

■ PRACTICE 98: Local Courts

Draw a line from each case in Column A to the correct court in Column B.

Column A

Column B

1. a theft of $90 in clothes from a village store

   a. divorce court

2. a citizen charged with tearing down a city neighbor's fence worth $200

   b. juvenile court

3. a 15-year-old charged with breaking the windows in a house

   c. small-claims court

4. a citizen who wants to end a marriage

   d. magistrate court

Special Districts

A **special district** is an area that is set up to take care of a specific service. Special districts are not part of any local government.

The school district is the most common kind of special district. The United States has over 14,000 school districts. These districts build and run schools. Their job is to make sure that children in their district get the best possible education.

Each school district is run by an elected school board. This board determines what will be taught in the district's schools. The school board decides on teacher salaries. The board also decides how much money each school will receive for books and other supplies. In many communities, school board members are volunteers—they are not paid for their work.

The chart below lists some other common types of special districts.

Type of District	In Charge Of
Water district	water supply
Public utility district	electricity, gas, and public transportation
Sanitation district	sewage and trash removal
Park and recreation district	parks and recreation centers

■ PRACTICE 99: Special Districts

Circle the letter of the correct answer to each of the following questions.

1. What does a school board do?
   a. runs a high school
   b. teaches different classes
   c. writes teaching lessons
   d. runs a school district

2. Which special district would be in charge of collecting your trash?
   a. sanitation district
   b. public utility district
   c. water district
   d. school district

Local Income

Local services cost money. How do local governments pay for these services? Some local governments charge taxes. These are mostly property taxes or taxes on licenses. Other local governments have sales taxes or income taxes. The state or federal government may also provide funds.

Users' fees often pay for many local services. Users' fees are charges placed on some local services. Money from parking meters, for example, may pay to fix sidewalks and roads. In some places, citizens pay water bills to cover the cost of water treatment.

Money from property taxes often goes to pay for local schools. Tolls are a special users' charge. For example, a city might charge drivers to cross a bridge or use a road. Money from this toll would be used to cover the cost of keeping the bridge or road in good condition.

■ PRACTICE 100: Local Income

Circle the letter of the correct answer to each of the following questions.

1. What type of tax provides most local government income?
   a. property taxes
   b. tolls
   c. income taxes
   d. state refunds

2. What is a toll?
   a. a special charge put on some local services
   b. a charge on the value of buildings and land
   c. a charge for crossing a bridge or using a road
   d. a tax on the money businesses make

Citizens and Local Government

Local government is the closest to direct democracy. It is easier for citizens to influence local government than state or federal government. Citizens can speak at a city council meeting or meet with local officials. Citizens can start petitions, or even run for office themselves. Citizens can work directly to make their communities better places in which to live.

Why do so many citizens get involved with local government? Local government affects people's everyday lives. Local services are important to everyone who lives in a community. Local government is also much smaller than state or federal government. So, many citizens feel more in touch with their local government. What's more, citizens can see the results of their actions more quickly at the local level.

TIP

Volunteering in local politics is one of the best ways to understand the terms and concepts in this lesson. Local government holds elections every year, and candidates are always looking for volunteers. Volunteers may be asked to help send out mailings, put up campaign posters, circulate petitions, or even get involved with running the campaign itself. If you are interested in volunteering, call the city or town clerk's office to find out when elections are held. The city or town clerk will also be able to provide you with a list of candidates. Then, call the candidate for whom you want to volunteer.

■ PRACTICE 101: Citizens and Local Government

Circle the letter of the correct answer to each of the following questions.

1. Why is local government closer to direct democracy than the federal government?
   a. Citizens are required to vote on all local issues.
   b. It is easier for citizens to influence local government.
   c. There is no strong leader in local government.
   d. all of the above

2. How can a local citizen make his or her opinion heard?
   a. by speaking at city council meetings
   b. by circulating petitions
   c. by running for office
   d. all of the above

3. Which of the following is NOT a reason why so many citizens get involved in local government?
   a. Local government affects everyone in a community.
   b. Citizens may feel more in touch with local government.
   c. Citizens want to make an impact at a national level.
   d. Citizens can see the results of their actions more quickly at the local level.

LESSON 26: County Government

WORDS TO KNOW

board of commissioners   divisions

community   parishes

counties   zoning ordinances

county seat

Kinds of Communities

A **community** is a group of people living in the same area. Every community is different. Towns and villages are small communities. Cities are larger communities.

Most towns, villages, and cities have some kind of government. These local governments provide many services for their communities. For example, local government may have a police force and a fire department. Local government may also be in charge of providing local drinking water and keeping it clean.

When the United States first became a country, most people lived on farms. The farms were spread over large areas. As a result, each state divided itself into **counties**. Each county had its own government.

Today, all 50 states still have counties, although some states use a different term. Louisiana calls its counties **parishes.** Alaska calls them **divisions.** In most states, counties are the largest units of local government. Counties help carry out state laws and services. (Connecticut and Rhode Island have geographic regions called counties. But their counties have no governing functions.)

■ PRACTICE 102: Kinds of Communities

Circle the letter of the correct answer to each of the following questions.

1. What is a county?
   a. a group of farms
   b. a form of local government
   c. a form of city government
   d. a farming government

2. How many states have counties?
   a. 50
   b. 49
   c. 48
   d. 47

Running County Government

Most counties elect a **board of commissioners.** (Sometimes it is called a *board of supervisors.*) This board has five to nine members. It is the legislative branch of the county government.

The county board has several jobs.

■ It passes county laws, called *ordinances.*

■ It sets county taxes.

■ It decides on a county budget. This determines which projects get money.

■ It works with county departments to carry out many local services.

County ordinances protect citizens. Health codes are ordinances that set health rules for public places. **Zoning ordinances** set rules for how land in the county is to be used—whether for farming, business, or housing.

Some county boards carry out both legislative and executive duties. But most counties elect a county manager or county president. He or she carries out the executive duties. These duties differ from county to county.

■ PRACTICE 103: Running County Government

Circle the letter of the correct answer to each of the following questions.

1. Which of the following terms describes county rules that say which areas must be used for farming?
   a. licensing requirements
   b. zoning ordinances
   c. health codes
   d. small claims

2. Which of the following is NOT done by a county's board of commissioners?
   a. trying cases in county court
   b. setting county taxes
   c. passing ordinances
   d. making a county budget

County Departments

As you know, a county's board of commissioners works with other county departments. These departments carry out many local services. Most counties have several officials who act as heads of county departments. Below is a list of the officials found in most county governments and the jobs they perform.

- The **county clerk** keeps county records (birth and death certificates, land sale records).

- The **recorder of deeds** handles property titles (shows who owns what land).

- The **county auditor** keeps track of the county's budget.

- The **county assessor** determines the value of land, homes, businesses, and buildings for tax purposes.

- The **superintendent of schools** may serve as the head of public schools in the county.

- The **district attorney** serves as lawyer for the county.

- The **county sheriff** enforces the laws of the county and state; runs the jail.

- The **county coroner** determines the causes of death.

■ PRACTICE 104: County Departments

Circle the letter of the correct answer to each of the following questions.

1. Which county officer keeps track of the county's budget?
   a. the county assessor
   b. the county clerk
   c. the county auditor
   d. the district attorney

2. Which county officer would you see to get your birth certificate?
   a. the county assessor
   b. the county clerk
   c. the county auditor
   d. the district attorney

Characteristics of Counties

Each state decides how many counties it will have. The number of counties is different from state to state. Texas, the second largest state, has the most counties—254. Delaware has only 3 counties. The largest state, Alaska, has 23. In all, the United States has about 3,142 counties.

The size of counties also varies. The largest county in the nation is San Bernardino County in California. It covers 20,064 square miles. Its area is larger than some states.

The smallest county in the United States is Kalawao County in Hawaii. It covers only 14 square miles.

Most counties have a **county seat.** This is the town or city in which the county's government offices are located. In most cases, all county offices are in one building. This building is the county courthouse. Most counties also have a jail.

■ PRACTICE 105: Characteristics of Counties

Circle the letter of the correct answer to each of the following questions.

1. Which of these statements about counties is TRUE?

    a. Most counties have their offices in one building.

    b. All counties are the same size.

    c. The largest states always have the most counties.

    d. All states have the same number of counties.

2. What is a county seat?

    a. the county jail

    b. the county's largest city

    c. the town or city in which the county's government offices are located

    d. the county's highest court

■ IN REAL LIFE

Everyone who lives in the United States lives in a county. Do you know the name of your county? Do you know what city in your county is the county seat? Find out by checking in your telephone book under the listings for county government. Write the information you find below.

Name of county _____

County seat _____

LESSON 27: City Government

GOAL: To understand the ways in which city government can be structured

WORDS TO KNOW

at-large members	city wards	strong-mayor system
city council	commissioner	weak-mayor system
city manager	mayor	

Running City Government

Within each county, there may be more than one city. Each city has its own local government. This is called *city government.*

Most cities elect a **mayor** and a **city council.** The mayor is the chief executive of city government. The city council is like a legislature. The city council usually has five to nine members. They are elected by **city wards,** or voting areas. Many city councils also have **at-large members.** These at-large members represent the whole city, not just one area. Together, the mayor and city council pass city ordinances. These laws run the city.

Who holds most of the power, the mayor or the city council? The answer differs from city to city. In some cities, the mayor has a lot of power. In others, the city council holds the most power.

Every city has many jobs that have to be done. The elected leaders cannot do all the work. City departments carry out many city services. Some common departments include the following:

- fire department

- police department

- sanitation department

- public transportation department

■ PRACTICE 106: Running City Government

Circle the letter of the correct answer to each of the following questions.

1. Which of the following is the term for a voting area within a city?
    a. city supervisor
    b. city council
    c. city ward
    d. city board

2. Which of the following is NOT a common city department?
    a. police department
    b. fire department
    c. sanitation department
    d. legislation department

The Weak-Mayor System

In some cities, the city council has most of the power. It passes laws. It makes the budget. It hires and fires city officers. The mayor is just another council member with a few extra jobs. Such cities have a **weak-mayor system.** Look at the diagram below.

Weak-Mayor System

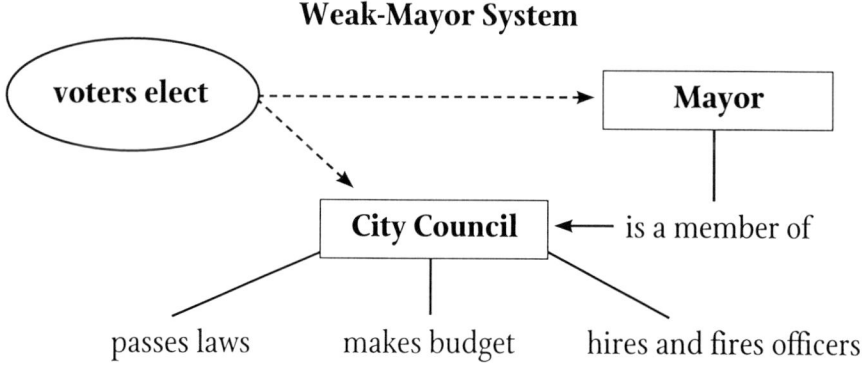

■ PRACTICE 107: The Weak-Mayor System

Circle the letter of the correct answer to each of the following.

1. Which of the following describes the mayor in a weak-mayor system?
   a. holds most of the power
   b. is not part of the city council
   c. is a city council member
   d. has no power at all

2. Which is a job of the city council in a weak-mayor system?
   a. to make the city budget
   b. to fire officers
   c. to pass laws
   d. all of the above

The Strong-Mayor System

In some cities, the mayor is very powerful. He or she is the true leader of the city. He or she can veto laws passed by the city council. He or she makes up the city budget. He or she chooses many city officers. The mayor may have as much power as some U.S. senators. Strong mayors are common in large cities. These cities have a **strong-mayor system**. Look at the diagram below.

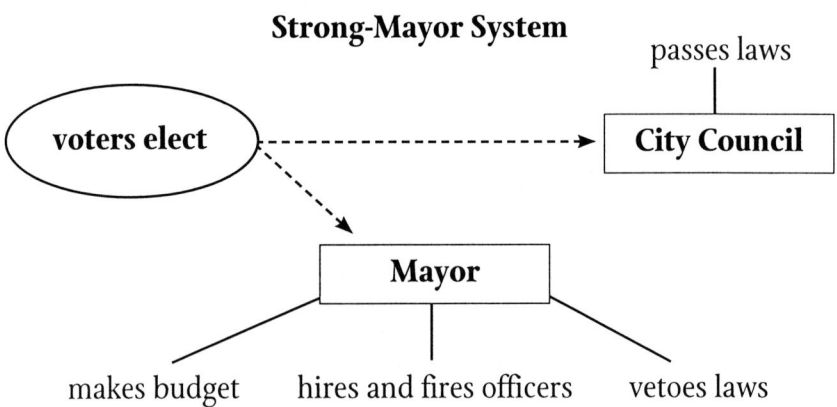

Strong-Mayor System

voters elect → City Council — passes laws

Mayor — makes budget, hires and fires officers, vetoes laws

■ PRACTICE 108: The Strong-Mayor System

Circle the letter of the correct answer to each of the following questions.

1. Who holds most of the power in a strong-mayor system?
   a. the city council
   b. the mayor
   c. the state legislature
   d. the board of commissioners

2. How is a city council in a strong-mayor system different from one in a weak-mayor system?
   a. The city council holds more power in a strong-mayor system.
   b. The city council holds less power in a strong-mayor system.
   c. They are the same.

The City Manager System

Some cities do not have a mayor. Instead, the city council hires a **city manager.** This manager is chosen because of his or her special management training. The city manager runs the everyday business of the city. For example, he or she may oversee city departments, such as the police or fire department. In this system, the city council has the same kind of duties and power as in a weak-mayor system. This type of city government is called a *city manager system.* Look at the diagram below.

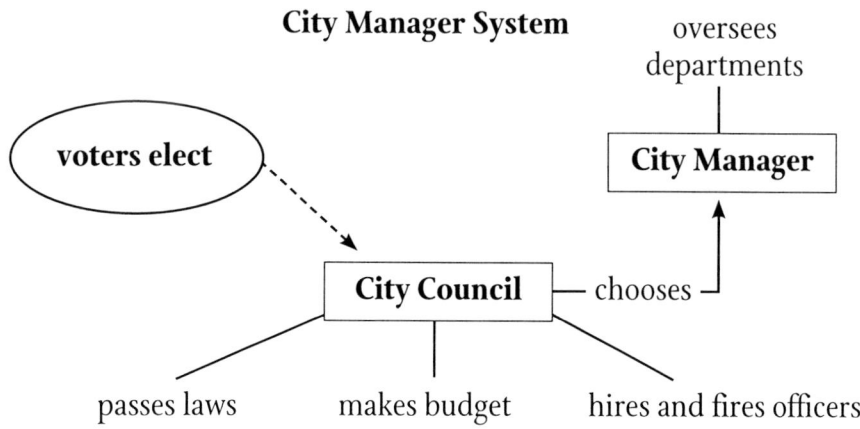

City Manager System

voters elect

oversees departments

City Manager

City Council — chooses

passes laws   makes budget   hires and fires officers

■ PRACTICE 109: The City Manager System

Circle the letter of the correct answer to each of the following questions.

1. What does a city council look for when it chooses a city manager?
   a. a popular personality
   b. a good voting record
   c. special management training
   d. experience as a lawmaker

2. In what way is a city manager like a weak mayor?
   a. He or she makes the budget.
   b. He or she vetoes city laws.
   c. He or she oversees departments.
   d. He or she fires officers.

The City Commission System

Some cities elect a board of commissioners. A board of commissioners is a group of officers. Each officer is called a **commissioner**. The commissioners do both legislative and executive jobs. As legislators, they pass ordinances and set up budgets. As executives, they may run different city departments. Small cities and towns often have this kind of city government. It is called a *city commission system*. Look at the diagram below.

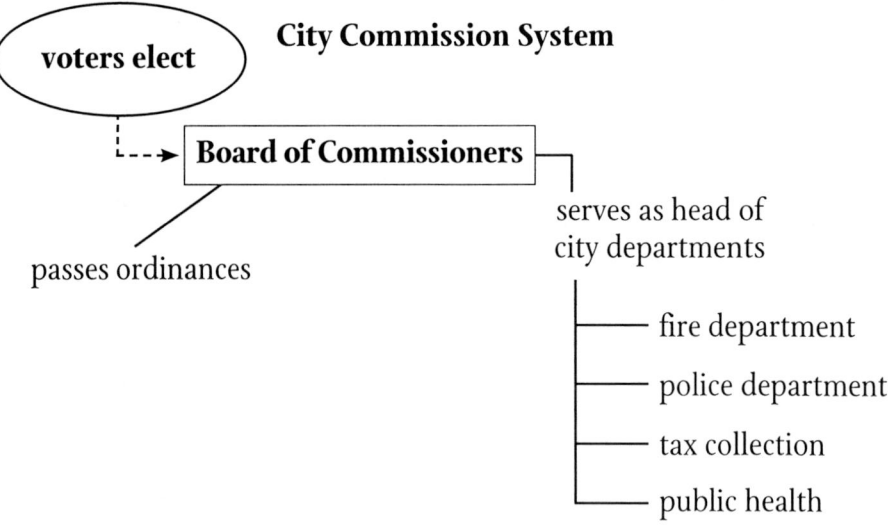

City Commission System

voters elect

Board of Commissioners

passes ordinances

serves as head of city departments

- fire department
- police department
- tax collection
- public health

■ PRACTICE 110: The City Commission System

Check each item below that names a duty of a board of commissioners.

☐ **1.** collecting taxes

☐ **2.** passing ordinances

☐ **3.** running the fire department

☐ **4.** choosing a city manager

TIP

You have just learned about four different systems of city government. To help you remember which is which, pay attention to the name of each system. This will help you remember the main feature of that system. For example, the weak-mayor system has a "weak mayor." The city commission system is run by a group of commissioners, and so on.

Four Types of City Government—Review

Here is a quick review of the four types of city government you have just learned about.

- The **weak-mayor system** has a weak elected mayor who shares power with the city council.

- In the **strong-mayor system,** an elected mayor has most of the power. This system is often found in large cities.

- The **city manager system** has a city manager who is not elected. The city manager runs the city's everyday business, but an elected city council has most of the power.

- The **city commission system** has a strong group of commissioners who act as both legislators and executives. This system is often found in small cities and towns.

■ PRACTICE 111: Four Types of City Government—Review

Write the correct type of city government on the line provided.

1. This type of city government has a chief executive who is not elected.

    _____

2. This type of city government has no chief executive.

    _____

3. This type of city government has a powerful, elected executive.

    _____

4. This type of city government has an elected mayor who shares power with the city council.

    _____

UNIT 7 REVIEW

Circle the letter of the correct answer to each of the following questions.

1. What is the largest area of local government?
    a. city
    b. county
    c. village
    d. town

2. What are the laws of a city or county government usually called?
    a. ordinances
    b. bills
    c. zones
    d. wards

3. What is the term for the city in which county government offices are located?
   a. township
   b. independent city
   c. county seat
   d. courthouse

4. Which level of government is closest to direct democracy?
   a. national
   b. state
   c. local
   d. federal

5. Which of the following actions can local governments NOT do?
   a. make state laws
   b. try people accused of breaking local laws
   c. run local programs
   d. raise local taxes

6. In which kind of city government is someone with special training hired to help run the city?
   a. city commission system
   b. city manager system
   c. strong-mayor system
   d. weak-mayor system

7. Which of the following local laws protects property?
   a. vandalism ordinances
   b. theft laws
   c. arson laws
   d. all of the above

8. Which type of judicial system has six different kinds of courts?
   a. justice
   b. magistrate
   c. municipal
   d. traffic

9. Which of the following is NOT an example of a special district?
   a. zone district
   b. school district
   c. public utility district
   d. water district

10. What is "home rule"?
    a. a form of state government
    b. a form of federal government
    c. a form of national government
    d. a form of local government

UNIT 7 APPLICATION ACTIVITY
In the News

It is important to stay informed about issues in your local government. These are the issues that will affect you most directly, whether it is the closing of a local school or a new tax on water treatment.

For one week, watch your local television news and scan your local newspaper. Pay attention to stories about issues that involve your town or community. On the lines below, list all of the local issues covered in the news during that week.

_____

_____

_____

_____

_____

_____

_____

_____

_____

_____

_____

_____

_____

_____

_____

_____

_____

_____

_____

_____

_____

_____

_____

_____

_____

_____

_____

_____

_____

_____

Now, choose the issue listed above that concerns you the most. Think about how this issue could affect your life. On another piece of paper, write a letter about this issue to the editor of your newspaper. Explain your opinion on the issue and how you think it should be resolved.

APPENDIXES

A. The Bill of Rights

Amendment I

Congress shall make no law respecting an establishment of religion, or prohibiting the free exercise thereof; or abridging the freedom of speech, or of the press; or the right of the people peaceably to assemble, and to petition the government for a redress of grievances.

Amendment II

A well regulated militia, being necessary to the security of a free state, the right of the people to keep and bear arms, shall not be infringed.

Amendment III

No soldier shall, in time of peace be quartered in any house, without the consent of the owner, nor in time of war, but in a manner to be prescribed by law.

Amendment IV

The right of the people to be secure in their persons, houses, papers, and effects, against unreasonable searches and seizures, shall not be violated, and no warrants shall issue, but upon probable cause, supported by oath or affirmation, and particularly describing the place to be searched, and the persons or things to be seized.

Amendment V

No person shall be held to answer for a capital, or otherwise infamous crime, unless on a presentment or indictment of a grand jury, except in cases arising in the land or naval forces, or in the militia, when in actual service in time of war or public danger; nor shall any person be subject for the same offense to be twice put in jeopardy of life or limb; nor shall be compelled in any criminal case to be a witness against himself, nor be deprived of life, liberty, or property, without due process of law; nor shall private property be taken for public use, without just compensation.

Amendment VI

In all criminal prosecutions, the accused shall enjoy the right to a speedy and public trial, by an impartial jury of the state and district wherein the crime shall have been committed, which district shall have been previously ascertained by law, and to be informed of the nature and cause of the accusation; to be confronted with the witnesses against him; to have compulsory process for obtaining witnesses in his favor, and to have the assistance of counsel for his defense.

Amendment VII

In suits at common law, where the value in controversy shall exceed twenty dollars, the right of trial by jury shall be preserved, and no fact tried by a jury, shall be otherwise reexamined in any court of the United States, than according to the rules of the common law.

Amendment VIII

Excessive bail shall not be required, nor excessive fines imposed, nor cruel and unusual punishments inflicted.

Amendment IX

The enumeration in the Constitution, of certain rights, shall not be construed to deny or disparage others retained by the people.

Amendment X

The powers not delegated to the United States by the Constitution, nor prohibited by it to the states, are reserved to the states respectively, or to the people.

B. The Declaration of Independence

IN CONGRESS, July 4, 1776.

The unanimous Declaration of the thirteen united States of America,

When in the Course of human events, it becomes necessary for one people to dissolve the political bands which have connected them with another, and to assume among the powers of the earth, the separate and equal station to which the Laws of Nature and of Nature's God entitle them, a decent respect to the opinions of mankind requires that they should declare the causes which impel them to the separation.

We hold these truths to be self-evident, that all men are created equal, that they are endowed by their Creator with certain unalienable Rights, that among these are Life, Liberty and the pursuit of Happiness.--That to secure these rights, Governments are instituted among Men, deriving their just powers from the consent of the governed, --That whenever any Form of Government becomes destructive of these ends, it is the Right of the People to alter or to abolish it, and to institute new Government, laying its foundation on such principles and organizing its powers in such form, as to them shall seem most likely to effect their Safety and Happiness. Prudence, indeed, will dictate that Governments long established should not be changed for light and transient causes; and accordingly all experience hath shewn, that mankind are more disposed to suffer, while evils are sufferable, than to right themselves by abolishing the forms to which they are accustomed. But when a long train of abuses and usurpations, pursuing invariably the same Object evinces a design to reduce them under absolute Despotism, it is their right, it is their duty, to throw off such Government, and to provide new Guards for their future security.--Such has been the patient sufferance of these Colonies; and such is now the necessity which constrains them to alter their former Systems of Government. The history of the present King of Great Britain is a history of repeated injuries and usurpations, all having in direct object the establishment of an absolute Tyranny over these States. To prove this, let Facts be submitted to a candid world.

He has refused his Assent to Laws, the most wholesome and necessary for the public good.

He has forbidden his Governors to pass Laws of immediate and pressing importance, unless suspended in their operation till his Assent should be obtained; and when so suspended, he has utterly neglected to attend to them.

He has refused to pass other Laws for the accommodation of large districts of people, unless those people would relinquish the right of Representation in the Legislature, a right inestimable to them and formidable to tyrants only.

He has called together legislative bodies at places unusual, uncomfortable, and distant from the depository of their public Records, for the sole purpose of fatiguing them into compliance with his measures.

He has dissolved Representative Houses repeatedly, for opposing with manly firmness his invasions on the rights of the people.

He has refused for a long time, after such dissolutions, to cause others to be elected; whereby the Legislative powers, incapable of Annihilation, have returned to the People at large for their exercise; the State remaining in the mean time exposed to all the dangers of invasion from without, and convulsions within.

He has endeavoured to prevent the population of these States; for that purpose obstructing the Laws for Naturalization of Foreigners; refusing to pass others to encourage their migrations hither, and raising the conditions of new Appropriations of Lands.

He has obstructed the Administration of Justice, by refusing his Assent to Laws for establishing Judiciary powers.

He has made Judges dependent on his Will alone, for the tenure of their offices, and the amount and payment of their salaries.

He has erected a multitude of New Offices, and sent hither swarms of Officers to harrass our people, and eat out their substance.

He has kept among us, in times of peace, Standing Armies without the Consent of our legislatures.

He has affected to render the Military independent of and superior to the Civil power.

He has combined with others to subject us to a jurisdiction foreign to our constitution, and unacknowledged by our laws; giving his Assent to their Acts of pretended Legislation:

> For Quartering large bodies of armed troops among us:

> For protecting them, by a mock Trial, from punishment for any Murders which they should commit on the Inhabitants of these States:

> For cutting off our Trade with all parts of the world:

> For imposing Taxes on us without our Consent:

> For depriving us in many cases, of the benefits of Trial by Jury:

> For transporting us beyond Seas to be tried for pretended offences

> For abolishing the free System of English Laws in a neighbouring Province, establishing therein an Arbitrary government, and enlarging its Boundaries so as to render it at once an example and fit instrument for introducing the same absolute rule into these Colonies:

> For taking away our Charters, abolishing our most valuable Laws, and altering fundamentally the Forms of our Governments:

> For suspending our own Legislatures, and declaring themselves invested with power to legislate for us in all cases whatsoever.

He has abdicated Government here, by declaring us out of his Protection and waging War against us.

He has plundered our seas, ravaged our Coasts, burnt our towns, and destroyed the lives of our people.

He is at this time transporting large Armies of foreign Mercenaries to compleat the works of death, desolation and tyranny, already begun with circumstances of Cruelty & perfidy scarcely paralleled in the most barbarous ages, and totally unworthy the Head of a civilized nation.

He has constrained our fellow Citizens taken Captive on the high Seas to bear Arms against their Country, to become the executioners of their friends and Brethren, or to fall themselves by their Hands.

He has excited domestic insurrections amongst us, and has endeavoured to bring on the inhabitants of our frontiers, the merciless Indian Savages, whose known rule of warfare, is an undistinguished destruction of all ages, sexes and conditions.

In every stage of these Oppressions We have Petitioned for Redress in the most humble terms: Our repeated Petitions have been answered only by repeated injury. A Prince whose character is thus marked by every act which may define a Tyrant, is unfit to be the ruler of a free people.

Nor have We been wanting in attentions to our Brittish brethren. We have warned them from time to time of attempts by their legislature to extend an unwarrantable jurisdiction over us. We have reminded them of the circumstances of our emigration and settlement here. We have appealed to their native justice and magnanimity, and we have conjured them by the ties of our common kindred to disavow these usurpations, which, would inevitably interrupt our connections and correspondence. They too have been deaf to the voice of justice and of consanguinity. We must, therefore, acquiesce in the necessity, which denounces our Separation, and hold them, as we hold the rest of mankind, Enemies in War, in Peace Friends.

We, therefore, the Representatives of the united States of America, in General Congress, Assembled, appealing to the Supreme Judge of the world for the rectitude of our intentions, do, in the Name, and by Authority of the good People of these Colonies, solemnly publish and declare, That these United Colonies are, and of Right ought to be Free and Independent States; that they are Absolved from all Allegiance to the British Crown, and that all political connection between them and the State of Great Britain, is and ought to be totally dissolved; and that as Free and Independent States, they have full Power to levy War, conclude Peace, contract Alliances, establish Commerce, and to do all other Acts and Things which Independent States may of right do. And for the support of this Declaration, with a firm reliance on the protection of divine Providence, we mutually pledge to each other our Lives, our Fortunes and our sacred Honor.

The 56 signatures on the Declaration appear in the positions indicated:

Column 1

Georgia:

Button Gwinnett

Lyman Hall

George Walton

Column 2

North Carolina:

William Hooper

Joseph Hewes

John Penn

South Carolina:

Edward Rutledge

Thomas Heyward, Jr.

Thomas Lynch, Jr.

Arthur Middleton

Column 3

Massachusetts:

John Hancock

Maryland:

Samuel Chase

William Paca

Thomas Stone

Charles Carroll of Carrollton

Virginia:

George Wythe

Richard Henry Lee

Thomas Jefferson

Benjamin Harrison

Thomas Nelson, Jr.

Francis Lightfoot Lee

Carter Braxton

Column 4

Pennsylvania:

Robert Morris

Benjamin Rush

Benjamin Franklin

John Morton

George Clymer

James Smith

George Taylor

James Wilson

George Ross

Delaware:

Caesar Rodney

George Read

Thomas McKean

Column 5

New York:

William Floyd

Philip Livingston

Francis Lewis

Lewis Morris

New Jersey:

Richard Stockton

John Witherspoon

Francis Hopkinson

John Hart

Abraham Clark

Column 6

New Hampshire:

Josiah Bartlett

William Whipple

Massachusetts:

Samuel Adams

John Adams

Robert Treat Paine

Elbridge Gerry

Rhode Island:

Stephen Hopkins

William Ellery

Connecticut:

Roger Sherman

Samuel Huntington

William Williams

Oliver Wolcott

New Hampshire:

Matthew Thornton

GLOSSARY

acquitted (uh-KWIT-ed) found not to be guilty

Administration (ad-min-is-TRAY-shun) the officials, especially cabinet members, who help the president run the executive branch of government

amendments (uh-MEND-munts) changes in the U.S. Constitution

anarchists (A-nur-kists) people who believe in anarchy

anarchy (a-NUR-kee) a situation in which there is no government

appeal (uh-PEEL) request that a verdict be overturned

appellate courts (uh-PE-lut KORTS) higher courts that decide whether lower-court trials were fair

articles (AR-ti-kuls) parts of the U.S. Constitution that describe the structure and workings of government

Articles of Confederation (AR-ti-kuls UV kun-fe-duh-RAY-shun) the first U.S. constitution, completed in 1777

at-large members (at-LARJ MEM-burz) members of a town or city council who represent the whole community, not just one neighborhood or district

attorney general (uh-TUR-nee JEN-rul) an officer who represents the state in court

ballot (BA-lut) the paper or card on which you mark your vote

bicameral legislature (by-KAM-uh-rul LE-jus-lay-chur) a legislature with two parts

bill (BIL) a proposed law

Bill of Rights (BIL UV RYTS) the first ten amendments to the U.S. Constitution; defines the rights of all U.S. citizens

board of commissioners (BORD UV com-MISH-uh-nurs) elected officials who run the government of a town or a city

branch of government (BRANCH UV GUH-vurn-munt) a major division of government

Cabinet (KAB-uh-nit) the body that advises the president, made up of the heads of 15 departments of the executive branch

candidate (KAN-duh-dayt) a person who has officially entered an election

case (CAYS) a court action

chamber (CHAYM-bur) an official meeting hall or room of one division of government (often within the judicial or the legislative branch)

checks and balances (CHEKS AND BA-luns-es) system that allows each of the three branches of government to balance the power of the other two branches

circuit courts (SUR-kut KORTS) second-highest system of courts

citizen (SIT-i-zuhn) a member of a community, such as a town, a state, or a nation

city council (SIT-ee KOWN-sul) a group of elected officials who share power for running a city or town government with a mayor

city manager (SIT-ee MA-ni-jur) a person with special management training hired to run the everyday business of a city

---

PRONUNCIATION KEY

CAPITAL LETTERS show the stressed syllables.

ng	as in running	u	as in but, some
o	as in cot, father	uh	as in about, taken, lemon, pencil
oh	as in go, note	ur	as in term
sh	as in shy	y	as in line, fly
th	as in thin	zh	as in vision, measure
oo	as in too		

city wards (SIT-ee WARDZ) voting areas within a city

civil case (SI-vul KAYS) a court case that involves a disagreement

coalition (KOH-uh-LI-shun) a group of parties or factions that band together to get more power

codes (KOHDZ) groups of laws that regulate special areas, such as health (health codes) or property (zoning codes)

colonists (KO-luh-nists) people living in a colony

colony (KO-luh-nee) a group of people living in a new territory who are still partially controlled by their home country

commissioner (kuh-MISH-uh-nur) an elected official who is in charge of one specialized area of city or town government

community (kuh-MYOO-nuh-tee) a group of people living in the same area

compromise (KOM-pruh-myz) a plan or an agreement that allows both sides on an issue to get some of what they want

Congress (KON-grus) the legislative branch of the U.S. government; includes the Senate and the House of Representatives

Constitution (kon-stuh-TOO-shun) a set of laws that serves as the highest law of the nation

constitutional (kon-stuh-TOO-shun-ul) legal because of agreeing with the U.S. Constitution

Constitutional Convention (kon-stuh-TOO-shun-ul kun-VEN-shun) a meeting held in 1787 to revise the Articles of Confederation

---

PRONUNCIATION KEY

CAPITAL LETTERS show the stressed syllables.

a	as in mat	f	as in fit
ay	as in day, say	g	as in go
ch	as in chew	i	as in sit
e	as in bed	j	as in job, gem
ee	as in even, easy, need	k	as in cool, key

constitutional monarchy (kon-stuh-TOO-shun-ul MON-ar-kee) a system of government in which the power is shared by elected officials and the king or queen

consumer (kun-SOO-mur) a person who buys and uses products and services

consumer protection (kun-SOO-mur pruh-TEK-shun) the government's efforts to keep people safe and treated fairly when they buy and use products

Continental Congress (kon-tun-EN-tul KON-grus) delegates who wrote the first U.S. constitution

convict (kun-VIKT) to find someone guilty of a crime

corporate tax (KOR-puh-rit TAKS) a charge put on the profits earned by companies doing business

counties (KOWN-teez) the largest divisions of local government

county seat (KOWN-tee SEET) the town or city in which a county's government offices are located

criminal case (KRI-muh-nul KAYS) a court case that involves a crime

Declaration of Independence (de-kluh-RAY-shun UV in-duh-PEN-duns) a document written in 1776 that declared the colonists' rights, reasons, and intentions to form a new nation

defendant (duh-FEN-dunt) a person who is accused of a crime or accused in a civil court case

delegated (DEL-uh-gay-tid) assigned authority to another body or person

---

PRONUNCIATION KEY

CAPITAL LETTERS show the stressed syllables.

ng	as in running	u	as in but, some
o	as in cot, father	uh	as in about, taken, lemon, pencil
oh	as in go, note	ur	as in term
sh	as in shy	y	as in line, fly
th	as in thin	zh	as in vision, measure
oo	as in too		

delegates (DE-li-guts) representatives; people sent to a meeting or gathering to represent other people

democracy (duh-MOK-ruh-see) a system of government controlled by the people, in which citizens vote on issues and/or their leaders

Democratic Party (de-muh-KRA-tik PAR-tee) one of the two major political parties in the United States

democratic process (de-muh-KRA-tik PRAH-ses) the system whereby voters in a democracy listen to different opinions, vote for representatives and issues, and abide by the results

despotism (DES-puh-tiz-um) a system of government completely controlled by one leader, in which citizens have no power

dictator (DIK-tay-tur) a person who rules a country by force (synonyms: tyrant, despot)

dictatorship (DIK-tay-tur-ship) a system of government completely controlled by one leader, in which citizens have no power

direct democracy (duh-REKT di-MO-kruh-see) a form of democracy in which citizens can vote on every issue

district courts (DIS-trikt KORTS) lowest-level federal courts

divisions (duh-VI-zhunz) in Alaska, the term used for counties

due process of law (DOO PRO-ses UV LAW) following the same fair rules in every criminal case

elect (uh-LEKT) choose by voting

PRONUNCIATION KEY

CAPITAL LETTERS show the stressed syllables.

a	as in m**a**t	f	as in **f**it
ay	as in d**ay**, s**ay**	g	as in **g**o
ch	as in **ch**ew	i	as in s**i**t
e	as in b**e**d	j	as in **j**ob, **g**em
ee	as in **e**ven, **ea**sy, ne**e**d	k	as in **c**ool, **k**ey

election (uh-LEK-shun) the process by which people vote to select someone for office

Electoral College (uh-LEK-tuh-rul   KAH-lij) the electors from all the states

electoral vote (uh-LEK-tuh-rul   VOHT) the vote of the Electoral College

electors (uh-LEK-turz) representatives from states chosen by voters to elect the president and vice president

eligible to vote (E-luh-juh-bul   TOO   VOHT) allowed to vote

enforces (en-FOR-siz) makes sure that laws are obeyed

executive branch (ig-ZE-kyuh-tiv   BRANCH) the part of government that enforces, or carries out, the law

Executive Compromise (ig-ZE-kyuh-tiv   KOM-pruh-myz) a compromise passed at the Constitutional Convention that limited the powers of the president

extreme (ik-STREEM) holding a view that is not in the middle; very strong

facts (FAKTS) statements that can be proved

federal budget (FE-duh-rul   BUH-jit) the national government's plan for earning and spending money over a certain period of time

federal government (FE-duh-rul   GUV-urn-munt) national government

federalism (FE-druh-li-zum) division of power between national and state governments

general election (JEN-uh-rul   uh-LEK-shun) the day on which citizens make their final vote for local, state, and national leaders

---

PRONUNCIATION KEY

CAPITAL LETTERS show the stressed syllables.

ng	as in running	u	as in but, some
o	as in cot, father	uh	as in about, taken, lemon, pencil
oh	as in go, note	ur	as in term
sh	as in shy	y	as in line, fly
th	as in thin	zh	as in vision, measure
oo	as in too		

general trial courts (JEN-rul TRY-ul KORTZ) state courts that handle serious cases

government (GUV-urn-munt) the people and system of rules that control a specific community of people

governor (GUH-vun-ur) an officer who heads the state's executive branch

Great Compromise (GRAYT KOM-pruh-myz) a solution passed at the Constitutional Congress of 1787 that created a Congress with two parts

guarantee (gar-un-TEE) a promise that something will be done exactly as described

home rule (HOHM ROOL) situation in which the power of local government is not limited by the state

House of Representatives (HAUS UV re-pri-ZEN-tuh-tivs) one of the two houses of Congress; membership based on a state's population

inauguration (i-naw-gyuh-RAY-shun) ceremony during which the winners of the presidential election are sworn into office as president and vice president of the United States

income tax (IN-kum TAKS) a charge on the money people earn

independents (in-duh-PEN-dunts) voters who do not join any political party

independent agencies (in-duh-PEN-dunt AY-jun-seez) government agencies that are not under the president's direct control and whose leaders are not part of the president's Cabinet

---

PRONUNCIATION KEY

CAPITAL LETTERS show the stressed syllables.

a	as in mat	f	as in fit
ay	as in day, say	g	as in go
ch	as in chew	i	as in sit
e	as in bed	j	as in job, gem
ee	as in even, easy, need	k	as in cool, key

inherent rights (in-HIR-unt RYTS) the right of all people to life, liberty, and the pursuit of happiness

initiative (i-NI-shuh-tiv) a proposed solution to a problem that is voted on by the people

interprets (in-TUR-pritz) makes the meaning of something clear for others

judicial branch (jyoo-DI-shul BRANCH) the part of government that interprets the law

jury duty (JUH-ree DOO-tee) a citizen's obligation to serve in court as a juror when asked

justice courts (JUS-tus KORTZ) in small communities, courts that try cases that are neither serious nor minor, such as burglaries

justices (JUS-tus-ez) judges, especially Supreme Court judges

law enforcement (LAW en-FORS-munt) making sure that laws are obeyed and that people who break laws are punished

legislative branch (LE-jus-lay-tiv BRANCH) the part of government that makes laws

legislature (LE-jus-lay-chur) an elected group of representatives who make the laws for a state or county

lieutenant governor (loo-TEN-unt GUH-vun-ur) elected state official who is ranked just below the governor and takes the governor's duties if he or she cannot perform them

local government (LOH-kul GUH-vurn-munt) government of a community below the state level

---

PRONUNCIATION KEY

CAPITAL LETTERS show the stressed syllables.

ng	as in runni**ng**	u	as in b**u**t, s**o**me
o	as in c**o**t, f**a**ther	uh	as in **a**bout, tak**e**n, lem**o**n, penc**i**l
oh	as in g**o**, n**o**te	ur	as in t**er**m
sh	as in **sh**y	y	as in l**i**ne, fl**y**
th	as in **th**in	zh	as in vi**s**ion, mea**s**ure
oo	as in t**oo**		

magistrate courts (MA-juh-strayt KORTS) in small communities, courts that try minor cases

majority (muh-JOR-uh-tee) the larger number; more than half of the votes that are cast

mandatory (MAN-duh-tor-ee) required

maximum security (MAKS-i-mum suh-KYUR-uh-tee) providing the greatest possible control over a community (such as a prison) to keep it, and others, safe

mayor (MAY-ur) an elected city leader

media (MEE-dee-uh) all modes of communication, such as radio, television, the Internet, newspapers, and so on

minimum security (MIN-i-mum suh-KYUR- uh-tee) providing the least possible control over a community (such as a prison) to keep it, and others, safe

minors (MY-nurz) those under the age of 18

moderate (MO-duh-rit) holding a view that is in the middle; not extreme

monarch (MON-ark) a person who inherits the power to rule a country

monarchy (MON-ark-ee) a government system with a monarch

municipal courts (myu-NIS-suh-pul KORTS) in cities, city courts of six kinds (civil, criminal, traffic, small-claims, juvenile, divorce)

national convention (NA-shuh-nul kun-VEN-shun) a large gathering in which party delegates choose their party's presidential candidate

---

PRONUNCIATION KEY

CAPITAL LETTERS show the stressed syllables.

a	as in mat	f	as in fit
ay	as in day, say	g	as in go
ch	as in chew	i	as in sit
e	as in bed	j	as in job, gem
ee	as in even, easy, need	k	as in cool, key

Glossary • American Government

New Jersey Plan (NOO JUR-see PLAN) a plan set forth by delegates from New Jersey at the Constitutional Congress for every state to have equal representation

opinions (uh-PIN-yunz) statements that cannot be proved

ordinances (ORD-uh-nuntz-ez) city or county laws

overrides (O-vur-RYDZ) the setting aside or overturning (of vetoes)

pardon (PAR-duhn) to formally forgive or excuse someone for having committed a crime or other offense

parishes (PAR-ish-ez) in Louisiana, the term used for counties

party delegates (PAR-tee DE-li-gits) representatives of a political party

petition (puh-TI-shun) a statement that is passed around for supporters to sign

plaintiff (PLAYN-tif) a person who accuses another of a crime; person who files a lawsuit in court

political party (puh-LI-ti-kul PAR-tee) a group that stands for certain issues or policies relating to government

popular vote (POP-yoo-lur VOHT) the vote of the people, versus the vote of the Electoral College

Preamble (PREE-am-bul) the introduction to the U.S. Constitution

precedent (PRE-suh-dint) what other judges have done in past cases

president (PRE-zuh-dint) the leader of the executive branch of U.S. government

---

PRONUNCIATION KEY

CAPITAL LETTERS show the stressed syllables.

ng	as in runni**ng**	u	as in b**u**t, s**o**me
o	as in c**o**t, f**a**ther	uh	as in **a**bout, tak**e**n, lem**o**n, penc**i**l
oh	as in g**o**, n**o**te	ur	as in t**er**m
sh	as in **sh**y	y	as in l**i**ne, fl**y**
th	as in **th**in	zh	as in vi**s**ion, mea**s**ure
oo	as in t**oo**		

primary elections (PRY-mar-ee i-LEK-shuns) special elections held in each state for choosing presidential candidates

prime minister (PRYM MIN-is-tur) the highest elected official in some democratic forms of government

principles (PRIN-si-pulz) basic rules or beliefs

prohibited (proh-HI-bi-tuhd) forbidden by law

property tax (PRO-pur-tee TAKS) a charge on the value of land and buildings people own

proposal (pruh-POH-suhl) a suggested plan

prosecutor (PRO-suh-kyoo-tur) a lawyer who argues a lawsuit in court on behalf of the plaintiff

protective services (pruh-TEK-tiv SUR-vis-ez) services that keep people safe and healthy

public works (PUH-blik WURKS) works done by the government on such things as roads, highways, bridges, parks, and public buildings

ratify (RA-tuh-fy) to pass, or approve

recall (ree-KOL) a vote to remove someone from office, following a successful petition

recommend (re-kuh-MEND) to advise in favor of something

referendum (re-fuh-REN-dum) a vote on a special issue

register to vote (RE-juh-stur TOO VOHT) to sign up to vote

regulate (REG-yoo-layt) to control

PRONUNCIATION KEY

CAPITAL LETTERS show the stressed syllables.

a	as in mat	f	as in fit
ay	as in day, say	g	as in go
ch	as in chew	i	as in sit
e	as in bed	j	as in job, gem
ee	as in even, easy, need	k	as in cool, key

representative democracies (re-pri-ZEN-tuh-tiv duh-MO-kruh-seez) forms of democracy in which citizens vote for representatives to decide issues

representatives (re-pri-ZEN-tuh-tivz) people elected to serve in the House of Representatives

Republican Party (ri-PUB-li-kin PAR-tee) one of the two major political parties in the United States

sales tax (SAYLS TAKS) a charge on goods people buy

secretary (SE-kruh-ter-ee) an official who is in charge of a specific area or department of government

secretary of state (SE-kruh-ter-ee UV STAYT) a state officer who keeps state records

self-government (SELF GUH-vurn-munt) government controlled by the people it serves

Senate (SE-nut) one of the two houses of Congress; includes two senators from each state

senator (SE-nuh-tur) a person elected to serve in the Senate

separation of powers (se-puh-RAY-shun UV POW-urz) the division of the U.S. government into three branches that share power

service (SUR-vis) the work done for, or benefits given to, members of a community

session (SE-shuhn) the time period when a group of officials meet and conduct business

---

PRONUNCIATION KEY

CAPITAL LETTERS show the stressed syllables.

ng as in runni**ng**	u as in b**u**t, s**o**me
o as in c**o**t, f**a**ther	uh as in **a**bout, tak**e**n, lem**o**n, penc**i**l
oh as in g**o**, n**o**te	ur as in t**er**m
sh as in **sh**y	y as in l**i**ne, fl**y**
th as in **th**in	zh as in vi**s**ion, mea**s**ure
oo as in t**oo**	

social welfare programs (SOH-shul WEL-far PROH-gramz) programs to help those in need

"sound bites" (SOWND BYTZ) short phrases or sentences that catch people's attention but do not convey much detail about real issues

special district (SPE-shul DIS-trikt) an area set up to take care of a special service

stable government (STAY-bul GUH-vurn-munt) an orderly government that can do its work and does not change frequently

stalemate (STAYL-mayt) a situation in which both sides of a debate, a game, or an issue are unable to win

state supreme court (STAYT suh-PREEM KORT) the highest state court

strong-mayor system (STRONG MAY-ur SIS-tum) form of local government in which the mayor has more power than the city council

Supreme Court (suh-PREEM KORT) the highest court in the United States

Three-Fifths Compromise (THREE-FIFTHS KOM-pruh-myz) a compromise passed at the Constitutional Convention; stated that a slave would be counted as three fifths of a free man

tolls (TOLZ) special user's charges, especially for roads and bridges

totalitarian state/totalitarianism (toh-ta-luh-TAR-ee-un STAYT) government that is controlled by one person

treasurer (TRE-zhuh-rur) a state officer who manages state money

---

PRONUNCIATION KEY

CAPITAL LETTERS show the stressed syllables.

a	as in mat	f	as in fit
ay	as in day, say	g	as in go
ch	as in chew	i	as in sit
e	as in bed	j	as in job, gem
ee	as in even, easy, need	k	as in cool, key

two-party system (TOO PAR-tee SIS-tum) a government with two major political parties

tyranny (TIR-uh-nee) government that is controlled by one person

unconstitutional (un-con-stuh-TOO-shun-uhl) not legal because of conflicting with the U.S. Constitution

unemployment pay (un-uhm-PLOY-muhnt PAY) money that is given by the state, for a certain period of time, to people who have lost their jobs

verdict (VUR-dikt) a decision announced by a jury about a defendant's guilt or innocence

vetoes (VEE-tohz) refuses to sign (a bill)

vice president (VYS PRE-zuh-dint) the second in command of the executive branch; serves as president if the president cannot serve

Virginia Plan (VUR-ji-nyuh PLAN) plan set forth by Virginia at the Constitutional Convention for representation according to population

voting bloc (VOH-ting BLOK) a group of political parties that join together for a certain amount of time in order to have more power in the government

weak-mayor system (WEEK MAY-ur SIS-tum) a form of local government in which the mayor has less power than the city council

zoning ordinances (ZO-ning ORD-uh-nuntz-ez) the rules for land use in a county or city

---

PRONUNCIATION KEY

CAPITAL LETTERS show the stressed syllables.

ng	as in running	u	as in but, some
o	as in cot, father	uh	as in about, taken, lemon, pencil
oh	as in go, note	ur	as in term
sh	as in shy	y	as in line, fly
th	as in thin	zh	as in vision, measure
oo	as in too		

INDEX

acquittals, 114
Adams, John Quincy, 134
Administration, 95
Alaska, 149
amendments, 27
    first ten. *See* Bill of Rights
    other, 48–49
    ratification of, 47
    rewriting, using your own words, 53–54
    steps for adding, 47
    voting, 71
American League, 130
American Party, 124
American Revolution, 32
    causes of, 34
anarchists, 4
anarchy, 4, 67
    in Somalia, 68
appeals, court, 104, 160
    reasons for, 106
appellate courts, 160
applications
    about your state, 172–173
    government in your own life, 23–24
    importance of voting, 81
    in the news, 200
    perfect president, 145–146
    rewriting amendments using your
      own words, 53–54
    your senators and representatives, 118
Argentina, 8
arson laws, 181
Articles of Confederation, 30
    problems with, 32
articles, of Constitution, 42, 44
at-large members, of city council, 192
attorney general, 157

balance of power flowchart, 115
ballots, 126. *See also* voting
bicameral legislature, 88
Bill of Rights, 42, 45–46, 202–203
    as heart of U.S. Constitution, 47

bills
    becoming laws, flowchart, 93–94
    committee recommendation of, 92
    introduction of congressional, 92
    last steps for, 93
    passage of, 94
board of commissioners, 188
board of supervisors, 188
branch of government, 85
budget, federal, 66
Bush, George W., 124, 127, 134, 135,
    138–139

Cabinet, 95
    departments and responsibilities of, 99
    secretaries, 99
candidates, 57
    learning about presidential, 140
    presidential, choosing of, 123
    researching information about, 75
    "sound bites" of, 141–142
    stands on issues of, 57
Capitol Building, 88
    meetings of Congress in, 89
cases, court, 105
caucuses, 123
cause and effect, 34
chambers, 88
charts
    organizing facts on, 141
    using, to compare and contrast ideas, 19
checks and balances, 40, 41, 111
    for Congress, 91
    in state government, 151
Chief Justice, 107
Child Online Protection Act (COPA), 112
circuit courts, 104, 160
    district courts, 104
cities, 178, 187. *See also* city government
    common departments of, 192
citizens, 5
    accepting results of elections, 69
    being informed, 140
    choosing of representatives by, 16

delegation of power by, 156
government by the people, as principle
  of, 38
inherent rights in, 39
interpretation of, by judicial branch, 108
key ideas in, 38
other principles of, 39
Preamble, 42
results from Constitutional
  Convention, 33
separation of powers, 39
spelling out of duties of Congress in, 90
steps to amending, 47
three main sections of, 42
Consumer Products Safety Commission, 100
consumer protection, 166–167
consumers, 166–167
context clues, using, 28
Continental Congress, 30
contrasting, 19
convictions, 114
corporate taxes, 162
counties, 178, 187
  characteristics of, 190–191
county assessor, 189
county auditor, 189
county clerk, 189
county coroner, 190
county courts, 160
county government
  county departments, 189
  running, 188
county seat, 191
county sheriff, 190
court cases, 105
  right to observe, 117
courts
  appellate, 160
  cases in, 105, 117
  circuit courts, 104, 160
  civil cases, 105, 107, 160, 182
  civil courts, 182
  county courts, 160
  criminal cases, 105, 107, 160, 182
  criminal courts, 182
  district courts, 104, 160

divorce courts, 183
federal courts, 103, 104
general trial courts, 160
justice courts, 182
juvenile courts, 160, 183
lack of, under Articles of
  Confederation, 30
of local governments, 182–183
magistrate courts, 182
small-claims courts, 183
state supreme courts, 160
structure of, 104
superior courts, 160
traffic courts, 182
crime, 68
crime labs, 168
crimes, 105, 160
criminal cases, 105, 107, 160, 182
criminal courts, 182
Czechoslovakia, 31
Czech Republic, 31

debates, 64
  held by political parties on issues, 66
  of issues at Constitutional
    Convention, 33
  of presidential candidates, 142
Declaration of Independence, 29, 39,
  204–207
  principles of, 29
  signatures appearing on, 208–209
defendants, 105
delegates, 30
  at Constitutional Convention, 33
democracy, 4
  democratic process and, 69
  differences between dictatorship and, 12
  direct, 15
    in states, 154–155
  examples of, 6
  features of, 5
  keeping strong, 116–117
  participating in, 70
  representative, 15, 16, 57, 64–65, 74
    with many political parties, 60
  separation of powers in, 39, 87

Supreme Court, 104. *See also*
Supreme Court
Federal Deposit Insurance Corporation (FDIC), 100, 101
federal government, 85
capital of, 85
enforcement of laws by executive branch of, 95
executive branch, 85
judicial branch, 85, 102–109
legislative branch, 85, 88. *See also* Congress
similarities between state government and, 151
federalism, 38
Federal Trade Commission (FTC), 100
fees, users', 184
Fifteenth Amendment, 48, 71, 107
Fifth Amendment, 45, 202
fire departments, 179
First Amendment, 45, 112, 164, 202
flag burning, 109
flowchart
balance of power, 115
of Electoral College system, 132
how bills become laws, 93–94
presidential election process, 129
foreign policy, 96
Fourth Amendment, 45, 202
freedom of religion, 164
freedom of speech, 108
lawsuit filed regarding, 112
limits to, 109

garbage collection, 179
general elections, 59, 125–127. *See also* elections; primary elections
holding of, 125–126
general trial courts, 160
geography, state, 149
Gore, Al, 127, 134, 135, 138–139
government
agencies affecting everyday lives, 101
arrest of U.S. citizens during World War II, 13
branch of, 85

definition of, 3
democracy, 4, 5
dictatorship, 4, 7–8
executive branch, 39
federal, 85
judicial branch, 39
lack of, in Somalia, 68
learning about, 74
legislative branch, 39
making working, 50–51
with many parties, 59
moderate versus extreme, 10–13
monarchy, 4, 6, 7
with one party, 61
by the people, 50
power divided between national and state, 38
power of, 64–65
principles of Declaration of Independence as foundation of U.S., 29
run by a coalition, 60
self-, 38
separation of powers, 39, 87
shutdown in 1996, 66
size of, 64
stable, 67
stalemates in, 66
with three branches, 39
three forms of, 13
types of, 4
of the United States, 27
weak national, under Articles of Confederation, 30
in your own life: application activity, 23–24
governors, 157
graphic organizer, state services, 169
Great Compromise, 33–34
Green Party, 59, 124

Harrison, Benjamin, 134
Hawaii, 149
Hayes, Rutherford B., 134
health codes, 181, 188
hospitals, local, 180
House of Representatives, 33, 88

duties of, 91
impeachment proceedings originating
in, 114
size of, 89
Speaker of, 98
state, 158

impeachment, 114
inauguration, presidential, 127
income taxes, 110, 162
independent agencies, 100
Independent Party, 124
independents, 59
index cards, 11
initiatives, 154
Internet, 47
internment, 13
issues
debated at Constitutional
Convention, 33
facing delegates at Constitutional
Convention, 33–34, 35, 36
of political parties, 66
regarding size and power of
government, 64–65
researching information about, 75
separating facts from opinions
regarding, 76–77
stands of candidates on different, 57
understanding different sides of, 74
voting on, 18
special, referendums, 154

Jackson, Andrew, 134
Jamestown, 29
Japanese Americans, 13
Johnson, Andrew, 114
Johnson, Lyndon B., 37
journalists, 19
judges, 86
judicial branch, 39, 85, 86, 102–109
checks on, 110–111
dispute settlement by, 102
duties of, 85
interpretation of Constitution by, 108
main duties of, 102–103

in state government, 151, 160
structure of, 161
jury duty, 152
justice courts, 182
juvenile courts, 160

Kennedy, John F., 138, 142

law enforcement, 168
laws
breaking of, 105
carrying out of state, 157
constitutional, 108
enactment of, 92–94
how bills become, flowchart, 93–94
interpretation of
by judicial branch of government,
102
state, 160
local, 181–182
made by state legislatures, 158
making and changing of, 38
mandatory seat-belt, 159
power of Supreme Court to strike
down, 40
unconstitutional, 108, 109
lawsuits, 112
lawyer, right to, 106
leaders, 5
voting to change, 12
legislative branch, 39, 85
checks on, 111–112
duties of, 85
in state government, 151, 158
legislatures
bicameral, 88
laws made by state, 158
Libertarian Party, 124
lieutenant governors, 157
local government, 177–186
citizens and, 185
counties as largest units of, 187. *See
also* county government
courts, 182–183
income for, 184–185
other services of, 180

powers of, 178
protective services provided by, 179–180
special districts, 183–184
types of laws under, 181–182
local hospitals, 180
lotteries, state, 162, 164

magistrate courts, 182
majority, 4, 5
citizen cooperation with, 69
majority opinion, 107
mandatory seat-belt law, 159
maximum security prisons, 168
May Day, 61
mayor, 192
media, 140
voters and, 141–142
minimum security prisons, 168
minority opinion, 107
minors, 112
Mississippi River, 149
moderate, 10
monarchs, 6
modern, 7
monarchy, 4
constitutional, 7
features of, 6
workings of, 13
municipal courts, 182–183

National Aeronautics and Space
Administration (NASA), 100
national conventions, 124
national government. *See* federal
government
National Guard, 156, 157
National League, 130
National Science Foundation (NSF), 100
Natural Law Party, 124
New Jersey Plan, 33
newspapers
gaining information on politicians
from, 19
getting facts about candidates from, 140
paying attention to words in, 118
reading, to learn about issues, 74

application activity, 200
Nineteenth Amendment, 49, 50, 71, 203
Ninth Amendment, 46
Nixon, Richard M., 114, 138, 142
notes, taking, 11

one-party system, 61
opinions, 59, 76–77
key words, indicating, 79
listening to different, in democracy, 69
oppression, 61
ordinances, 181, 188
city, 192
override, 40, 93

pardons, 157
parishes, 187
Paris, Treaty of, 32
park and recreation districts, 184
party delegates, 124
Perón, Evita, 8
Perón, Juan, 8
Perot, Ross, 126
petitions, 154
plaintiffs, 105
police departments, 179
political parties, 57, 157. *See also*
two-party system
candidates of, 57
choosing of presidential candidates by, 123
different systems of, 62
issues debated by, 66
joining, 59
national conventions held by, 124
representative democracies with
many, 60
in the United States, 124. *See also*
two-party system
politicians, 19
popular vote, 126
electors and, 131
winning, but losing election, 134,
138–139
population
and Electoral College, 136–137
House of Representatives based on, 33

representatives
   application activity, 120
   attend Continental Congress, 30
   at Constitutional Convention, 32
   in House of Representatives, 33
   in primary elections, 124
   replacing, 17, 38
   responsibilities of, 50–51
   in Senate, 33
   state, 149
   supporting citizens' interests, 69
   terms of, 90
   voting for, 16
Republican National Convention, 124
Republican Party, 59, 124
resources, of states, 149
rights, 12
Rocky Mountains, 149

sales taxes, 162, 184
sanitation districts, 184
school boards, 183
school districts, 183
schools
   private, 164
   public, 164
Second Amendment, 45, 202
secretaries, Cabinet, 99
secretary of state, 157
self-government, 38
Senate, 33, 88
   approval of Supreme Court justices, 107
   duties of, 91
   size of, 89
   state, 158
senators, 89
   application activity, 120
   number of, from states, 89, 126
   terms of, 89
separation of powers, 39, 87
   for Congress, 91
   in state government, 151
sequence of events, 34
services, 162
sessions, 88
Seventh Amendment, 46, 203

sewage treatment, 180
Simpson, O.J., 107
Sixteenth Amendment, 49, 110
Sixth Amendment, 45, 202
slavery, 35, 71
   made illegal by Thirteenth
     Amendment, 48
slaves
   counting of, 35
   denial of vote to, 71
slave trade, 35
Slovakia, 31
Socialist Party, 59
Socialist Party USA, 124
Socialist Workers Party, 124
social welfare programs, state, 165
   paid for through taxes, 166
Somalia, 68
South Vietnam, 37
Soviet Union, 31
   Communist Party in, 61
Speaker of House, 98
special districts, 183–184
   common types of, 184
stable government, 67
stalemate, 66
state governments
   branches of, 151
   checks and balances in, 151
   citizen control of, 152
   constitutions, 149, 153
   consumer protection provided by, 166–167
   costs of, 162–163
   education provisions of, 162, 164
   executive branch, 151, 157–158
   judicial branch, 151, 160
   law enforcement services provided by, 168
   legislative branch, 151, 158
   paying for services for, 162–163
   powers of, 38, 156
   prisons run by
     maximum security, 168
     minimum security, 168
   public works, 167

unconstitutional, 108
unemployment pay, 165
United Kingdom, 7
United Nations, 68
United States. *See also* Constitution, U.S.
    and England, difference of spelling in, 43
    government, 27
    principles serving as foundation of, 29
    shutdown in 1996, 66
    internment of Japanese Americans in, 13
    justice system, 106
    as representative democracy, 16
    as two-party system, 59
    voting blocs in, 60
users' fees, 184
U.S. Postal Service, 101

vandalism laws, 181
Venn diagrams, 19
verdicts, 106
vetoes, presidential, 40, 93
    overriding of, 93
vice president, 95
    duties of, 97–98
Vietnam War, 37
villages, 178, 187
Virginia Plan, 33
visualizing, 19
volunteering, 186
voter registration, 75–76
voters, media and, 141–142
voting
    age lowered to eighteen by Twenty-
        sixth Amendment, 49
    amendments, 71
    application activity, 81
    to change leadership, 12
    citizens and, 74
    eligibility, 72
    importance to citizens of, 50, 74, 152
    reasons for not, 78
    registration, 75–76
    for representatives, 16
    responsibilities of, 70
    as right and responsibility, 78

rights
    denial of, 71
    given to all men, in Fifteenth
        Amendment, 48
    for women, in Nineteenth
        Amendment, 49
    on special issues, 154
voting bloc, 60

War of Independence, 32
Washington, D.C., 85
    Capitol Building, 88, 95
    meeting of Supreme Court in, 107
    White House, 85, 95
water districts, 184
Watergate scandal, 114
water treatment, 179
weak-mayor system, 193, 197
White House
    as president's home, 85, 95
    staff, 95
witnesses, right to call, 106
Workers World Party, 124
The World Almanac, 47
World Series, 130
World War II, 13

zoning ordinances, 188